Excellence

How to Pursue an Excellent Spirit

By Andrew Wommack

Harrison House

Tulsa, OK

20 19 18 17   10 9 8 7 6 5 4 3 2 1

Excellence: How to Pursue an Excellent Spirit
ISBN: 978-1-68031-174-7
Copyright © 2017 by Andrew Wommack Ministries

Published by Harrison House Publishers.

Contents

Introduction

Everyone loves promotion. But for many, promotion seems to be an elusive thing. Why is that? What causes some workers to be promoted over others? What makes a boss look favorably on certain employees? Is there a "magic formula" to promotion? Can promotion be guaranteed?

I believe it can.

Though some people think promotion only comes to those with the education and charisma to back it up, and others feel that managers promote based on friendships or special connections, the Bible says something completely different:

> *For promotion cometh neither from the east, nor from the west, nor from the south. But God is the judge: he putteth down one, and setteth up another.*

Psalm 75:6-7

Promotion comes from God. It is not an arbitrary thing. It doesn't travel from the east or west like the wind. It's not random. It is God who exalts. But did you know that He is not the one who determines whether or not you're promoted?

You may be thinking, *Wait, Andrew; you just contradicted yourself. First you said promotion comes from God, but then you said that He doesn't determine if I'm promoted.*

Both of those statements are correct. God is not the one who determines whether or not we receive promotion. God created each of us for success. He doesn't "sovereignly" make some people leaders and others followers. He has big plans for each of us (Jer. 29:11) but we have total choice (Deut. 30:19).

Some people believe that they were born "duds." Maybe you're one of them. Maybe you feel like you don't have the talents and abilities needed for promotion and success. Even if you've experienced failure in the past, I'm telling you on the authority of God's Word, you were made for more!

God doesn't make junk (Ps. 139:14). He created you for greatness. If you're working at a business, God wants you to be the best worker there. If you're a farmer, God will give you wisdom to grow better crops at a higher profit. If God has called you to be a mother, do it with all your heart. Show the world the blessing of a godly heritage (Eph. 6:7). Whatever realm you're in, God has created you to succeed (Deut. 28:13).

Some people call this an American gospel, but it's just the Gospel. I've preached this message in remote areas of Africa and seen it work. Prosperity and promotion, though relative to what God has called each person to do, is available to every born-again believer.

We have to get past the mindset that we can't succeed. It doesn't matter how much money we make or where we live. It doesn't matter who our parents are or the color of our skin.

It doesn't matter how we've failed in the past or what talents or education we think we're missing. We all have the potential for greatness—if for no other reason than because the Spirit of Christ dwells within us (Rom. 8:9-11). But potential is not enough. I once heard a man say that the place with the most potential is a graveyard. He's right. Graveyards are full of people who never reached their full potential and took it to the grave with them. Potential isn't enough to guarantee promotion; we have to discover the missing link.

Chapter One

The Key to Promotion

We don't have to attend the "school of hard knocks" in order to gain wisdom and find success. Many scriptures in the Bible teach us how to live well on the earth. For instance, 1 Corinthians 10:11 says that the lives of the Old Testament saints were recorded as examples for us. If we take the time to learn from their life stories—both the good and the bad—we can avoid some of the pain that comes when learning through trial and error.

In the book of Daniel, we see that Daniel and his three Hebrew friends gained promotion in an evil, ungodly society. Though they were captives from Israel, considered the lowest class of society in Babylon, they grew in favor and influence with four kings in two different world systems to become trusted advisors and rulers. How was that possible? How could these four men experience so much favor in so many different circumstances? The answer can be found in Daniel 6:

> *Then this Daniel was preferred above the presidents and princes, because an excellent spirit was in him; and the king thought to set him over the whole realm.*

Daniel 6:3

Like his three friends, Daniel was promoted because he had an excellent spirit. The phrase "excellent spirit" only appears in the book of Daniel, yet the concept can be found throughout the Bible. (By the way, this word *spirit* isn't talking about a part of someone's makeup, like spirit, soul, and body; it's referring to an attitude.) Though the terminology differed in various instances, Jesus often spoke of the importance of having an excellent spirit: "He that is faithful in that which is least is faithful also in much: and he that is unjust in the least is unjust also in much" (Luke 16:10).

In another instance, Jesus illustrated the concept with a parable. As a master was preparing to leave on a journey, he entrusted some of his wealth to three servants according to their abilities. While the master was away, his servants managed his wealth. Two of the servants doubled their master's investment, but the third hid his money in the ground (Matt. 25:14-18). When the master returned, he called his servants to account for what they had done with his money. The two servants who made a profit were rewarded and promoted by their master: "His lord said unto him, Well done, thou good and faithful servant: thou hast been faithful over a few things, I will make thee ruler over many things: enter thou into the joy of thy lord" (Matthew 25:21, see also Matt. 25:23). But the lazy servant was cast out:

> *His lord answered and said unto him, Thou wicked and sloth-ful servant, thou knewest that I reap where I sowed not, and gather where I have not strawed: Thou oughtest therefore to have put my money to the exchangers, and then at my coming I should have received mine own with usury. Take therefore the talent from him, and give it unto him which hath ten talents. For unto every one that hath shall be given, and he shall have abundance: but from him that hath not shall be taken away even that which he hath. And cast ye the unprof-itable servant into outer darkness: there shall be weeping and gnashing of teeth.*

Matthew 25:26-30

Many people read this story and think that the master was harsh or unfair in his treatment of his servants. But they forget that the money each servant had really belonged to the master. The master, therefore, had a right to do with it as he pleased. He chose to give each servant a portion of his money with the understanding that they should *"occupy till* [he] *come"* (Luke 19:13, brackets added).

The master wasn't unfair; he understood his servants' abilities and entrusted his money to them accordingly. I'm sure he also considered the possibility that he could lose some money. But when he returned and brought his servants before him to give an account, something about the lazy servant's response made him angry. His anger couldn't have been over the physical loss of money because the servant hadn't lost anything. The master's anger must have been kindled by something intangible; I believe it was the servant's attitude. In this parable, it was the servant's attitude that got him fired. Attitude is important. It can get you fired, or it can get you promoted. Let's take a look in Genesis to see how Joseph's attitude got him promoted.

Joseph's life started out good. He was the favored son of his father and enjoyed privileges that made his brothers jealous. They hated Joseph and eventually sold him into slavery in Egypt. Yet in the midst of these horrible circumstances, Joseph had an excellent spirit. He didn't complain or pout. He just served his master with a good attitude, as if he were serving God. Before long, Joseph's master put him in charge of the entire household. Though the master's wife eventually lied about Joseph and had him thrown in prison, even there, Joseph's good attitude helped him rise to the top. Eventually Joseph caught the attention of Pharaoh, and was promoted to second in command of the mightiest nation on the earth. All of his advancement came because Joseph had an excellent spirit (Gen. 37-45).

We see this same spirit of excellence in Moses, David, and other Old Testament patriarchs. They believed God for something more, and because they all had an attitude of faithfulness and a spirit of excellence, they were all promoted.

Sadly, today many Christians don't believe God for anything. They shoot at nothing and hit it every time! Heroes of faith like Daniel, Joseph, Moses, and David were different. If we want to experience the results they had, we have to start doing the things they did. We have to start aiming at something.

David believed God for more. When all his brothers were cowering before Goliath, he looked beyond who he was in the natural—the youngest son of Jesse from the smallest town in Judah—and focused on his covenant with God. Even when everyone questioned David's ability to fight Goliath, pointing to Goliath's superior size and experience, David kept his confidence in God. First Samuel 30:6 says that David "encouraged himself in the Lord." He remembered keeping his father's sheep on the backside of the desert. He remembered being attacked by a lion and a bear and slaying them. He remembered God's faithfulness in those circumstances and said, "This uncircumcised Philistine shall be as one of them" (1 Sam. 17:36-37).

David's father sent him into the hills to protect the sheep. He might have even told David to fight off threatening animals. But no one, not even his father, would have blamed David for losing one little sheep to a lion or bear. His father wouldn't have wanted David to risk his life protecting the sheep. No father would. But David had an excellent spirit. He was faithful in the little things—even when no one was watching. And those relatively small victories gave him the confidence he needed to face Goliath.

I remember when Jamie and I were called into the ministry, and I quit my secular job. For six years, I pastored three little churches in Texas and Colorado. The first one had a maximum of 12 people in attendance, the second might have gotten up to 50, and the third averaged 100 people every Sunday (in a town with a population of 144 people). But my vision was much bigger than that. I saw myself ministering to people all over the world. What I saw in my heart, and what was actually happening in the flesh, was so different that I walked around in a constant state of conflict and tension. Yet I knew I had to remain faithful. I knew I couldn't despise the day of small beginnings (Zech. 4:10).

I've seen other people in similar situations who wanted to minister to millions. They said, "Put me in charge. I'll be faithful. Give me a church of a thousand; I'll be an awesome pastor." Yet they wouldn't even give themselves completely to a Sunday school class or Bible study group. That's not the way it works. Remember what Jesus said: Only those who are faithful in that which is least will be faithful with much (Luke 16:10).

Though the temptation to give less than my best was there, I knew God was calling me to be faithful. So I preached to five people like they were 5,000. I gave each of those churches everything I had. I really believe that this attitude solidified an excellent spirit inside me and allowed God to promote me to where I am today.

You see, everyone wants the benefits of promotion. They like the recognition and influence that comes with it. But how many are willing to do the things Joseph, David, Daniel, and Daniel's three Hebrew friends did? How many are willing to be faithful, even in the small things that no one sees? How many will keep a good attitude in the face of difficult circumstances? How many will remain true to their convictions, even when it hurts? Who will develop an excellent spirit? This is the key to promotion.

Chapter Two

A Heart Issue

Most people, unfortunately, settle for less than what God has called and equipped them to be. Even I have been guilty of this. On January 31, 2002, the Lord spoke to me from Psalm 78:41. He told me I was limiting Him by my small thinking. At that time, I knew God had called me to do some of the things I'm doing now through television and media, but in my heart, I didn't see myself doing them. I didn't classify myself with the "big dogs." I enjoyed flying under the radar and dodging the bullets of criticism that other ministers had to deal with.

I had seen a measure of success; our ministry was touching lives and miracles were happening—my own son was even raised from the dead! Yet I still hadn't fully embraced God's calling for my life. I didn't see myself reaching the multitudes, even though everything God was speaking to me was pushing me in that direction.

I was frustrated. Things didn't seem to be working out like they should, and the reason lay in my own heart: I had settled for less. When I determined to take the limits off God, our ministry exploded with growth! Within ten years, the number of people responding to our message (through phone calls and website visits) increased over 1,000 percent! Requests for material increased nearly 5,000 percent!

Today, we're reaching people all across the globe. Our *Gospel Truth* television program is broadcast to a potential 3.2 billion people every day, and we're on most networks. Our Bible school in Colorado is bursting at the seams. We're doing everything we can to take the message of God's grace as far and deep as possible, and we're seeing tremendous results. But this only happened when I dealt with my heart and stopped settling for less than God's best.

I believe this is a process we all have to go through. You know life, especially religious life, tends to be easier when we take the path of least resistance. With everything we experience and all the junk perpetrated in the news, it's easier to settle. It's easier to be sick. It's easier to fear. It's less work to be fat and dumb. It's less work to complain. It's easier to just go with the flow. Even doctors gravitate toward "easy" when they give their patients the very worst-case scenarios and say things like, "We don't want to get your hopes up."

We need to get our hopes up! Hope is the thermostat of faith. We need faith. We need a goal. The problem is, most of us have been taught to motivate ourselves with the negative. For instance, if a person wants to lose weight, instead of surrounding himself with pictures of someone slim and fit (positive motivation), he puts up pictures of someone fat (negative motivation). In the same way, instead of meditating on going to work, doing a good job, and being promoted, most people force themselves to go to work so they can pay their bills and keep their families from starving to death.

The whole world's system gravitates toward the negative. But that just breeds mediocrity and teaches people not to get their hopes up or believe for big things. God created us differently. Therefore, we shouldn't act, talk, and think like the world does. We're not of this world (John 17:14-16).

Our society as a whole (Christians included) has mastered doing what's right only when someone is watching. But that is not the attitude of a person with an excellent spirit! I read an article in *Reader's Digest* recently about a social experiment conducted on honesty. Testers planted a "lost" wallet in several different cities around the world. Each wallet had the equivalent of $50, along with photos and contact information inside. The testers hid around the corner, watching to see how many people would attempt to do the right thing and reunite the wallet with its owner. Unfortunately, the majority of people picked up the wallet, looked around to see if anyone was watching, and then pocketed the money. When the experimenters caught up with the people and asked them why they didn't attempt to contact the person whose information was in the wallet, the people said they figured nobody would know. In other words, they weren't worried about getting caught, so they didn't do what they knew was right.

Getting caught has nothing to do with doing what is right! Yet our society has bought into the lie that morality is relative, while excellence is overrated. People think that as long as nobody gets hurt, or as long as number one is taken care of, it doesn't matter what they do. But that's wrong! The truth is, God's standard does not change (Num 23:19). What was wrong fifty years ago is still wrong today, and the things that are right today will be right 1,000 years from now.

Christians who know God's standard should be like cream that rises to the top. Our excellence—our attitudes—should lift us well beyond our peers in government, in business, in family, and in every area of our lives. Our attitude determines our altitude!

It amazes me how many people pray for promotion and increase, yet have bad attitudes. They don't realize that their attitudes, though intangible, are still very noticeable. For example, people notice if you're stressed. They notice when you're excited. It's not just physical cues that give you away; there is a spiritual connection between your heart attitude and your actions.

I once met a guy in Phoenix, Arizona, who worked for a church where I was speaking. He was assigned as my driver, and for the five days I was there, even though he wanted me to sit in the backseat, I sat up front with him and tried to start a conversation. He would answer direct questions but no matter what I said, I couldn't get him to engage in a conversation. It was obvious that he did not enjoy his job. He had a horrible attitude. On the last day I finally asked, "What's wrong with you? I can tell you're not happy. What's going on?"

This guy opened up and began sharing with me that he came to this large church because he thought they would give him more opportunities to minister. He was preaching somewhere else, but he felt he needed a steppingstone to fulfill God's purpose and reach more people. This church was supposed to be his steppingstone. He was angry because the only thing he had done since being hired was chauffeur people around.

I said, "I don't understand why they won't let you preach. Why wouldn't they want you to open your mouth and spew this bad attitude? Why wouldn't they want to infect their people with your bitterness and anger?"

He just sat there stunned for a minute. I said a little more gently, "Don't you see? It's your attitude that's holding you back. You may feel justified, but if you allow offenses and bitterness to thrive in you and discouragement to have its way, you will limit what God can do in your life."

If you are going to see promotion, you have to maintain a good attitude, regardless of what other people do to you and regardless of circumstances. I don't have any way to prove this because I'm not moving backwards in the things God has called me to, but if for some reason I lost this ministry and had to go work at McDonald's, it would only be a matter of time before I started prospering. Why? Because I maintain an excellent spirit. I would go to that minimum wage job praising God for His provision, and I'd work there with all my heart. Before long, I believe I would be the manager of that business. And then the owner. Soon I'd own an entire chain of McDonald's, not because I knew the right person or had amazing management skills, but because that's what's in my heart. My attitude would promote me.

An excellent spirit will promote you in business, in ministry, or at home with your family. It will promote you among your neighbors, in your school, or at city council meetings. There are no limitations to an excellent spirit. God delights in excellence, but excellence starts in the heart. If you aren't being promoted, if it seems like everyone else is prospering while you struggle to make ends meet, or if you feel like you've been passed over for a promotion, it may be that you don't have an excellent spirit. Your heart attitude could be hindering you from living out God's best for your life. Proverbs 23:7 says, "For as [a man] thinketh in his heart, so is he" (brackets added). It is the attitude of the heart that prompts your actions. Jesus said:

A good man out of the good treasure of his heart bringeth forth that which is good; and an evil man out of the evil treasure of his heart bringeth forth that which is evil: for of the abundance of the heart his mouth speaketh.

Luke 6:45

Change cannot happen externally until it first happens internally. Fighting the pervasive mediocrity of the world and changing your heart attitude is impossible on your own. It takes a supernatural ability that you don't have, unless you've been born again. But being born again is more than just believing that God exists. James 2:19-20 says:

Thou believest that there is one God; thou doest well: the devils also believe, and tremble. But wilt thou know, O vain man, that faith without works is dead?

Being born again requires the grace of God (which He's already given) and our active faith (Eph. 2:8). Faith is more than just believing. Faith is active. It does something with what it believes. If you've merely believed that there is a God, you've done nothing more than what Satan has done. To be born again, you've got to do something the devil has never done—you have to act on your faith and submit your life to Christ. Romans 10:9 says, "Confess with thy mouth the **Lord** Jesus, **and** ... believe in thine heart" (emphasis added).

Belief is not enough. You must bow your knee and make Jesus your Lord. It's a commitment—not that you'll never fail, because that is impossible—but that you're willing to let Christ and His Word rule your life. It's not magic. It's not a question of whether or not God can forgive you. Grace has already been poured out. Jesus has already died, risen, and forgiven you. The question is, will you surrender? Will you add your faith to His grace? Will you make Him Lord?

Chapter Three

The Power of Choice

According to the psalmist, promotion comes from God (Ps. 75:6-7), as does salvation, healing, provision, and every other good thing in our lives (Ps. 103 and James 1:17). Yet we all know people who are not saved or healed. We all know some-one—or we might *be* that someone—who isn't experiencing promotion and provision. Is God playing favorites? Does He choose to bless some people and not others? Of course not! God is not a respecter of persons (Rom. 2:11). According to Matthew 5, God provides for every one of us equally, even the unbeliever!

For he maketh his sun to rise on the evil and on the good, and sendeth rain on the just and on the unjust.

Matthew 5:45

Titus says that God's grace, His goodness, has appeared to every person (Titus 2:11). So why isn't everyone saved? Why isn't everyone healed? Why isn't everyone being promoted? Could it be that not everyone knows these amazing gifts are available to them (2 Pet. 1:3)? Or more likely, could it be that not everyone has chosen to respond to God's grace with faith?

God does not force His goodness upon anyone. Promotion, like salvation and healing, is available to every person on the face of the planet. But not everyone will experience it for the same reason that not everyone experiences salvation or healing: They have not chosen to respond to God's grace with active faith.

*Now unto him that is able to do exceeding abundantly above all that we ask or think, **according to the power that worketh in us**, Unto him be glory in the church by Christ Jesus throughout all ages, world without end. Amen*

Ephesians 3:20-21, emphasis added

Before God's will can come to pass in our lives, we must cooperate. By grace, God has provided salvation, healing, provision, favor, acceptance, excellence, and every other thing we need to live the abundant life He promised us through Christ (2 Pet. 1:3 and John 10:10). But we can only experience this abundant life "according to [to the extent of] the power [or faith] that worketh in us" (brackets added). In other words, it is not automatic.

God always gives people the power of choice (Deut. 30:19). He will never force anyone to go to heaven. He will never force anyone to live by the power of His Spirit. If you don't want to be healed, God will let you stay sick. If you don't want to prosper,

God will let you stay poor. But if you want to receive all the blessings and promises of God—including promotion—you can!

Jesus said, "Fear not, little flock; for it is your Father's good pleasure to give you the kingdom" (Luke 12:32). God desires for each of us to experience His good will. But the only way to do that is to "seek first His kingdom," like Luke 12:31 says. We have to choose to do things God's way.

> *But rather seek ye the kingdom of God; and all these things shall be added unto you. Fear not, little flock; for it is your Father's good pleasure to give you the kingdom.*
>
> ### Luke 12:31-32

Though it goes against popular culture, the way up in God's kingdom is down. In God's kingdom, giving is better than receiving (Acts 20:35). God's way is to love your enemies and bless those who curse you (Matt. 5:44). In God's kingdom, the prerequisite for greatness is servanthood (Mark 10:44).

> *Servants, be obedient to them that are your masters according to the flesh, with fear and trembling, in singleness of your heart, as unto Christ; Not with eyeservice, as menpleasers; but as the servants of Christ, doing the will of God from the heart; With good will doing service, as to the Lord, and not to men.*
>
> ### Ephesians 6:5-7

Though most of us can't relate to the master-servant relationship these verses talk about, nearly all of us can apply this concept to the relationship between an employer and employee.

It can also apply to our civic, family, and church relationships. No matter what situation we find ourselves in, whether on the job, at church, or in our families, Paul said that we should serve those in authority over us "as unto Christ" and "not with eye service."

Many people serve their bosses or their families with eye service: They only work hard or do the right thing when someone is watching. Everything they do is done to impress people. But someone with an excellent spirit serves from the heart, as if they were directly serving the Lord. It may seem counterintuitive to work hard and not get the credit, but a person with an excellent spirit knows that God is their source. They aren't worried about pleasing people. Because of that, they will receive their reward directly from God.

Knowing that whatsoever good thing any man doeth, the same shall he receive of the Lord, whether he be bond or free.

Ephesians 6:8

It doesn't matter if you work for a good company or a bad one. It doesn't matter if people recognize you or not. It doesn't matter if you're the boss or the lowest person on the totem pole. If you have the right heart attitude—if you choose to have an excellent spirit—God will see it and He will reward you "whether [you] be bond or free" (brackets added).

You may be thinking, *That won't work in my situation. My boss is terrible. There's no possibility of promotion at my job.* There are multiple ways God can bless and promote you. For example, it may be that doing your job "heartily, as to the Lord" (Col. 3:23) causes another business to see your attitude and work ethic and hire you out from under your current boss. Or perhaps God will give you your own business. I don't know how it will happen, but I do know that this is a promise of God, and God keeps His promises (Jer. 1:12)!

One time a man came to me griping about what it was like to work for an ungodly boss. He complained about helping his boss's business prosper, while repeatedly being passed over for promotions. He said, "I've been with this guy since the beginning. I was the only employee he had for years. Now new people are coming in, and their starting salaries are more than mine. He's promoting them over me. It's just not fair. I've got more seniority." He just kept going on and on.

It was hard to listen to him, so I finally interrupted him and asked, "Who'd want to promote this rotten attitude? You've got a terrible attitude. You're criticizing your employer and your employment when you ought to be blessing it. You know, when Jesus only had a little boy's lunch to feed thousands of people, He didn't curse it. He didn't tell His disciples, 'This isn't enough! What were you thinking?' He never said, 'This isn't going to work.' Jesus took what He had and gave thanks. He blessed the five loaves and two fish and then used them to feed the multitude. There were even enough leftovers for dinner [John 6:1-13]!"

I dealt with this man for some time about blessing what he had and about forgiving his boss and praying for him. Two weeks later, this man was working on a project when his boss came through railing on him about some trivial thing. But the man had been praying, so without thought, he turned and said, "I forgive you."

His boss was taken aback. "Forgive me?" he asked. "What are you forgiving me for?"

The man replied, "I've been bitter toward you. I was your first employee, and now you've got all these other employees you're promoting over me. I've felt wronged, so I've had a bad attitude. I'm sorry. I'm forgiving you for the things I feel have been done wrong to me, and I'm asking you to forgive me for my attitude."

The man's boss became even more upset, and he yelled and stomped off. But after a while, he came back and started asking questions. This man got to minister to his boss and was awed when he began opening up about his own problems. Eventually the boss said, "I'm sorry. I've been dealing with a lot of personal problems and I've taken it out on you."

The two men became friends and within a short period of time, the man I spoke with was promoted above everyone else in the company. His pay was doubled, and the boss even gave him two weeks of paid vacation. God turned the whole situation around because this man chose to have an excellent spirit.

I know that your situation may be different, but you have to start somewhere. Start with what you have. Bless it, cooperate with God, and watch His goodness overtake you (Deut. 28:2). I have seen this truth work over and over again. It doesn't matter if you work for a large company or a small company. It doesn't matter if you have a good boss or a bad boss. It doesn't matter if you're a construction worker or a government employee. It doesn't even matter if the "right person" knows your name. If you change your attitude and choose to have an excellent spirit— whether others see it or not—God will see it and reward you!

Here's another example of how God promoted someone with an excellent spirit. The man who is now CEO of Andrew Wommack Ministries, Paul Milligan, once worked in a large secular company with multiple people over him. Though Paul worked with excellence, it didn't look like anyone would ever know who he was. Then Paul's direct supervisor took notice of Paul's work and began stealing his ideas and presenting them to management as his own. Paul's ideas caused the company to prosper, but he never got credit for them. Instead, Paul watched as his supervisor got promotions, raises, and bonuses because of his ideas.

At that point, Paul made a choice. Instead of getting angry, he took Ephesians 6:5-8 and made a commitment to keep working with excellence "as to the Lord." He trusted that God would promote him. Nearly a year later, another supervisor came to Paul and started asking questions. "Did you come up with this idea?" he asked. "How about this one? And this one?"

Paul answered truthfully, "Yes, I did."

"We knew that it had to be you," he said. "It couldn't have been your supervisor, he's not that smart."

So, they took Paul and made him his old supervisor's boss. But even then, Paul didn't lord his position over his old supervisor. He continued to work with excellence and as a result, was promoted many times. Paul eventually prospered so much that he started his own companies. He is now in the process of selling one of his companies for tens of millions of dollars—all because he chose to have an excellent spirit!

Chapter Four

The Power of Identity

Choosing to have an excellent spirit means choosing to live like Daniel and his three Hebrew friends. Even though these men were ripped from their homeland and made slaves in a godless society, their faithfulness and excellence prospered and promoted them and eventually made them rulers over the very ones who had taken them captive.

In the book of Daniel, Israel has been conquered by pagan King Nebuchadnezzar. As members of Israelite nobility, young Daniel, Hananiah, Mishael, and Azariah were taken from their homes and forced into the king's service. It's quite likely that these men were made eunuchs and that many of their friends (and maybe even their parents) were killed in front of their eyes. These men were then immersed in a pagan system and taught its laws, language, and culture, and even pressured to worship its gods.

> *And the king spake unto Ashpenaz the master of his eunuchs, that he should bring certain of the children of Israel, and of the king's seed, and of the princes; Children in whom was no blemish, but well favoured, and skilful in all wisdom, and cunning in knowledge, and understanding science, and such as had ability in them to stand in the king's palace, and whom they might teach the learning and the tongue of the Chaldeans. And the king appointed them a daily provision of the king's meat, and of the wine which he drank: so nourishing them three years, that at the end thereof they might stand before the king. Now among these were of the children of Judah, Daniel, Hananiah, Mishael, and Azariah.*

Daniel 1:3-6

For three years, Daniel and his friends were groomed to serve King Nebuchadnezzar as Chaldean (Babylonian) wise men. Since Babylon was conquering nations and growing so quickly, there weren't enough educated men to run the government. So the king began taking young, handsome men from countries he invaded and taught them the history and laws of Babylon that "they might stand before the king" and advise him.

Daniel and his friends were chosen because of their youth, appearance, and aptitude. But to serve the king, they were expected to discard their former identity and adopt the pagan identity of Babylon. Everything about these men reflected their heritage and their relationship with God—even their names. According to *Strong's Concordance*, the name Daniel means "judge of

God," Hananiah means "Jah has favored," Mishael's name asks "Who (is) what God (is)?" and Azariah's name declares "Jah has helped."

The king's official was given a very specific job. He was to strip these men of their Jewish identity and refashion them into Babylonians, starting with their names:

Unto whom the prince of the eunuchs gave names: for he gave unto Daniel the name of Belteshazzar; and to Hananiah, of Shadrach; and to Mishael, of Meshach; and to Azariah, of Abednego.

Daniel 1:7

I find it interesting that though the Babylonians had many gods and even incorporated other people's gods into their everyday lives, they did not recognize or reverence the God of Israel. They ignored the one true God to the extent that Daniel and his three friends were given new names that reflected the false gods they were expected to adopt. Yet these four Hebrew men never forgot that they were Jews. Though they stood alone without family, friends, or country, they never cast aside their covenant with God. I'm sure it would have been easier to go with the flow and convert, yet they remained faithful. They continued to obey God's laws and even called themselves by their Hebrew names (Dan. 1:8 and 2:17).

This is an awesome example of our directive in Romans 12:

And be not conformed to this world: but be ye transformed by the renewing of your mind, that ye may prove what is that good, and acceptable, and perfect, will of God.

Romans 12:2

Other translations of Romans 12:2 say, "Do not imitate this world" (The Original Aramaic New Testament in Plain English), "Do not follow the customs of the present age" (Weymouth New Testament), and "Don't copy the behavior...of this world" (New Living Translation). Daniel, Hananiah, Mishael, and Azariah did not allow themselves to be conformed to or molded by the Babylonian system. Neither should we.

Satan tries to force us to adapt to the world's way of thinking. He wants us to struggle with unbelief and relegate morality to an outdated tradition with no place in everyday life. But if we want to experience the good things of God to the extent that it changes our lives and causes promotion, then each of us has to pursue an excellent spirit.

At my sister's funeral, I was blessed by the number of people who spoke of her love for the Lord. It seemed like everyone had a story about how my sister, Joyce, had impacted them or led someone else to the Lord. It was a wonderful tribute. But after the funeral, text messages started popping up complaining that the service focused too much on Jesus and not enough on Joyce. Finally, one of my relatives texted back, "You can't talk about Joyce without talking about Jesus!"

Joyce's identity was so locked up with Jesus that it was nearly impossible to separate one from the other. I wish that could be said of every one of us. As believers, we're called to "be conformed to the image of [God's] Son" (Rom. 8:29, brackets added), not the image of the world. We have to renew our minds to the point that our identity is in Christ, or we'll never develop an excellent spirit.

Many people only know themselves in the natural. They base their identity on external, natural things. But Daniel, Hananiah, Mishael, and Azariah's identities went beyond what the Babylonians could see and beyond youth, beauty, and aptitude. These men knew they were more.

If I were to ask a group of people to identify themselves, most would respond by telling me their name or giving me their job description. They'd say, "I'm John, and I'm a carpenter," or "My name's Sally, and I'm a young mom with two kids." Some people might even try describing what they look like: "I'm short ... I'm athletic ... I wear glasses." But this shortsighted application of identity can be dangerous. What happens if John gets hurt and can no longer work as a carpenter? What happens when Sally ages or when the athlete loses a game? Without a deeper understanding of identity, people can experience what psychologists call an "identity crisis."

Even if someone were to include personality traits, like being outgoing or shy, in their identity, they would still be working from an incomplete definition. We are more than what we can see or feel. We are more than natural beings. God created us in His image as three-part beings. We are a spirit, we possess a soul, and we live in a body (Gen. 1:27 and 1 Thess. 5:23). Though most people agree with this statement theoretically, they struggle to understand it functionally.

Everyone understands what the body is. We see it, hear it, touch it, and smell it every day of our lives. Our bodies are constantly receiving and responding to stimuli. We know when our bodies are hot or cold, when they're short of fuel, and we even know when they get tired.

Most people also recognize the presence of a soul, which is made up of the mind, will, emotions, and conscience. Most people refer to the soul as the personality. Like the body, the soul is clearly identifiable even though it is unseen. It is the part of us that makes decisions, solves problems, empathizes with strangers, and defines right and wrong. It houses our memories and processes our experiences. We know when the soul is scared or hurt. We know when it's happy or sad. We know because we *feel* it. But we cannot feel the spirit.

The spirit is the part of us created in the image of God (Gen. 1:27). The spirit communicates with God and gives life to the body (John 4:24 and 6:63). But the spiritual part of us cannot be contacted in any physical, natural way. That's why most people believe the spirit and soul to be one inseparable part. Yet Hebrews clearly tells us this is not the case:

> *For the word of God is quick, and powerful, and sharper than any twoedged sword, piercing even to the dividing asunder of soul and spirit, and of the joints and marrow, and is a discerner of the thoughts and intents of the heart.*

Hebrews 4:12

Only the Word of God can separate spirit and soul for us. Only God's Word can show us the "more" of our identity. Most people think of their identity as the characteristics or traits that define them and make them different from everybody else. But when I looked it up, I discovered that identity is actually made up of those traits that make us the *same* as somebody else.

According to the *American Heritage Dictionary*, the word "identity" comes from the Latin word *idem* and means "the same" (Second College Edition, s.v. "identity"). We were created in the image of (the same as) God—a spirit. Through Adam and Eve's disobedience, we lost that identity. But when we were born again, we were made brand new!

Therefore if any man be in Christ, he is a new creature: old things are passed away; behold, all things are become new. And all things are of God, who hath reconciled us to himself by Jesus Christ, and hath given to us the ministry of reconciliation.

2 Corinthians 5:17-18

All things aren't *becoming* new, and they don't just have the *potential* to be new. They *are* new. Right now. And "all things are of God." What part of us is "of God"? What part was changed to be the same as He is? The body? The soul? No. After the new birth, we still look and think the same. We still have the same eye color and the same size feet. We still have the same memories. The part that changed was our spirit.

A new heart also will I give you, and a new spirit will I put within you: and I will take away the stony heart out of your flesh, and I will give you an heart of flesh.

Ezekiel 36:26

33

Therefore we are buried with him by baptism into death: that like as Christ was raised up from the dead by the glory of the Father, even so we also should walk in newness of life.

Romans 6:4

Our spirits were recreated in the image of God. We were made brand new from the inside out. Our new identity is one that is *idem,* the same, as Christ's (Rom. 8:29 and Eph. 4:24). We are more than what we can see or feel. We are the children of God (Gal. 4:4-7)!

But this new identity can sit dormant within us if we don't acknowledge who we are in Christ.

That the communication of thy faith may become effectual by the acknowledging of every good thing which is in you in Christ Jesus.

Philemon 6

Daniel and his friends knew they belonged to God, even after they were snatched out of their own country and had probably seen their parents, relatives, and friends killed. Living in an oppressive system under the control of an ungodly dictator, Daniel and his friends refused to conform to the customs and behaviors of the world around them. They knew who they were. Their God-identity protected them through the trials and temptations of Babylon, just like Jesus' identity protected Him in the wilderness.

The Gospels of Matthew and Luke record the temptation of Jesus. While there's a lot we can learn from that experience, I want to point out one aspect that many people miss. In chapter four of both Matthew and Luke, Satan approached Jesus twice with these words: "If thou be the Son of God..." (Matt. 4:3, 6; Luke 4:3, and 9).

Some people think Satan was genuinely curious as to whether or not Jesus was the Son of God. They think Satan was asking Jesus to prove Himself so that he would know he wasn't wasting his time on the wrong guy. But I don't think so. I believe Satan's goal was to get Jesus to doubt who God said He was (Matt. 3:17 and Luke 3:22).

Satan had used that same trick on Adam and Eve in the Garden of Eden. When the serpent told Eve that if she ate of the forbidden fruit she would be like God, he was trying to get her to doubt who God said she was (Gen. 3:5). Eve was already like God (Gen. 1:26) because she was created in His image. The first Adam sinned because he didn't know his identity. The last Adam, Jesus, didn't sin because He knew His identity. That's powerful! What you don't know *can* hurt you.

Chapter Five

The Power of Relationship

The key to having an excellent spirit and experiencing all the other benefits of your salvation is knowing who you are in Christ, not just who you are in the natural. Even if you are one of the most beautiful and talented people on the planet, your beauty and talent will only take you so far.

In a way, I pity the people the world favors, because it's so easy for them to depend on their own abilities or to base their identity on their outward qualities. Eventually talent runs out, beauty fades, or someone "more beautiful" arrives to take the more prominent place.

On the other hand, when you don't have a lot of natural things going for you, you quickly learn to lean on who you are in Christ. That's what happened in my life. All my life I've been average—never the best, never the worst. Everything I did growing up turned out average. Mediocre. It became part of who I was. Because of that, I found myself settling for average even after I was saved.

My experience with the Lord on March 23, 1968, however, started a process that changed my identity. I began to recognize that I was a new person in Christ and that the limits imposed on me because of my abilities were removed. I've explained these truths God showed me in *Spirit, Soul & Body*, but before I understood them, I only knew myself by what I saw in the mirror. I was an introvert. I wasn't a leader. I knew I couldn't look someone in the face and talk to them, so I didn't even try. I knew my limitations, and I let them put a ceiling on what I could do. But today I talk to millions of people. My wife says I could even talk to a fence post! This isn't because my natural tendencies have changed; it's because I've discovered my true identity.

Verily, verily, I say unto you, He that believeth on me, the works that I do shall he do also; and greater works than these shall he do; because I go unto my Father.

John 14:12

In 1968, I realized that I'd been made a brand-new person in Christ, and with Christ, I could do anything (Phil. 4:13). I started believing I could see blind eyes and deaf ears opened. I started believing I could see people raised from the dead. I started believing everything I saw in the Word was possible. And when I started believing, I started seeing those things happen.

If you're going to have an excellent spirit, if you're going to believe for promotion and for something more than average, you're going to have to identify who you are in Christ. You're going to have to go beyond your natural talents and abilities. I know that's a shock to many people, but it's true.

For ye see your calling, brethren, how that not many wise men after the flesh, not many mighty, not many noble, are called: But God hath chosen the foolish things of the world to confound the wise; and God hath chosen the weak things of the world to confound the things which are mighty; And base things of the world, and things which are despised, hath God chosen, yea, and things which are not, to bring to nought things that are: That no flesh should glory in his presence.

1 Corinthians 1:26-29

God delights in choosing people who can't do it in the natural. As a matter of fact, if you're only doing what you can do with your own talents and abilities, then I doubt you've found God's will for your life. God will call you to do something that is beyond yourself, beyond your abilities, so that "no flesh should glory in his presence," and no one can say, "Look what I've done."

I once received a letter from a man who knew he'd been called into the ministry, but he couldn't figure out why God chose him. He didn't have any special abilities. He didn't have any special connections. Even his wife struggled with the idea and said, "You could never be a minister. And there's no way I'm going to be a minister's wife." The two of them actually divorced over this, and for twelve years, this man floundered through life as he tried to come to terms with his calling.

At one of my meetings, he finally quit fighting. He later sent me a letter that said, "After seeing God use you to minister and open blind eyes, I've determined that God can use me. I've decided to go into full-time ministry." Further down in his letter, he asked, "Why is it that God uses hicks from Texas to preach His Word? He's used you and Copeland and Hagin. Why do you have to be a hick for God to use you?"

I wrote back, "It's because hicks from Texas know their success has got to be from God!" I know this bothers a lot of people because they think that if God can use a person with no talent, He ought to really be able to use someone with lots of talent. But too many talented people think, *Oh God, I can see Your wisdom in choosing me. I'll be such an asset. I'll make this easy. You just get me introduced, you get me on stage, and I'll take it from there.*

From God's standpoint, no matter how many talents a person has, no one is worthy to represent Him. No flawed human being could adequately represent an infinitely perfect God. In ourselves, none of us are good representatives of the Creator of the universe.

After I was called into the ministry, there was a time when Jamie and I struggled financially. We would go days without food. We drank water because it was free. We rarely filled up our gas tank because we just couldn't afford it.

I remember going to a conference when Jamie was eight months pregnant. While we were there, we heard a teaching on biblical prosperity. It was the first time we had ever heard that message, and we desperately needed to hear it again, but we just couldn't afford the materials. We had not eaten in days. We ran out of gas on the way there. We literally had nothing.

As I watched my wife struggle to hold back tears of disappointment, I promised the Lord that if He ever gave me a revelation that could help others, I would never deny them access to it because of their lack of finances.

I've learned a lot since those early days of ministry and marriage, but when Jamie and I first started out, I didn't know how to run a multimillion-dollar ministry. I struggled to run my own household budget! Yet, today our ministry is flourishing. We touch millions of homes with the Gospel. We see healings and miracles regularly. Every year we give away hundreds of thousands of dollars' worth of product. We have a building in Colorado Springs worth about $7 million, and we're building a first-class Bible college campus in Woodland Park, Colorado, that's going to cost a couple hundred million dollars. (At the time of this writing, we've already completed over 70 million dollars' worth of the project completely debt free.) God has done amazing things, and there's no way I can take credit for any of it!

I know that I am nothing in myself. When people look at me or hear my accent, they don't think, *Wow, he's awesome!* Instead, they look right through me and see what our ministry has accomplished and think, *Wow, God is awesome!* I'm convinced this is part of the reason God has chosen me to accomplish these things.

I remember the first time I ever saw Kathryn Kuhlman minister. I was still part of the Baptist church at the time, and I had been taught against women preachers, so I went to her meeting prejudiced about the whole thing. When she came out on stage, I knew my prejudice was right. She was strange! Everything about her turned me off.

She wore long, flowy dresses with crazy sleeves that she used like wings. She would flit out on stage and wave her arms about. She used an affected accent, turning God's name into three syllables and saying things like "Me thinks I hear ...." There was nothing about Kathryn Kuhlman I liked. But she was used of God.

The first time I saw her was when I had signed up to be an usher at one of her meetings. The fire code required there be clear access to emergency exits, so my job was to make sure people weren't blocking the aisles. This meant that people in wheelchairs and stretchers had to be moved to safe locations, sometimes without their equipment. I remember taking a woman off a stretcher and carrying her to a chair. She looked like a Holocaust victim, all bones and skin; she had to have weighed less than a hundred pounds. She could barely lift her own hand. Yet during the meeting, I saw her get up, run down the aisle, and jump on stage. I remember watching in awe as she pushed her own stretcher around the room.

I saw many other miracles that night. I saw blind eyes and deaf ears opened. But mostly, I saw God use a woman who, in my mind, was a weak, despised thing. All I could do was give God the glory.

Chapter Six

It's Personal

You've heard it said that God doesn't have any grandchildren. It's true. You can't inherit a relationship with God like you inherit a house. It has to be personal. You have to develop your own personal relationship with Him.

Daniel, Shadrach, Meshach, and Abednego each had a personal relationship with God. They didn't consider themselves Jews simply because their parents or grandparents were Jewish. Neither did they follow God's Law just to fit in with everyone around them. If they had, it would have been easy for them to compromise when circumstances became ugly. Instead, these four men made their faith personal.

I believe that before Daniel and his friends got to Babylon, they had already made the decision to follow God. They already knew who they were. They already knew the Word. They had an internal compass showing them right and wrong, giving them purpose and direction. That knowledge saved their lives.

Brothers and sisters, life is so much easier when you prepare. Just like road trips can be pleasant when you have a map, and questions aren't stressful when you know the answers, battles of faith are not scary when you know who wins. Unfortunately, many believers never get personal with their faith. They don't know who they are or what they believe. They only communicate with God and open His Word in crisis situations. Trust me when I tell you that a battleground is not the place to learn to shoot a gun—you'll get yourself killed!

But Daniel purposed in his heart that he would not defile himself with the portion of the king's meat, nor with the wine which he drank: therefore he requested of the prince of the eunuchs that he might not defile himself.

Daniel 1:8

Notice that Daniel "purposed in his heart." He made a faith decision *before* going into battle. If Daniel and his friends had not made their faith personal *before* they got to the king's table, we would have never heard of them. They would have become one more statistic that proved the corruption of Babylon. Instead, the moment they made the decision not to defile themselves, they won the battle of compromise.

Now God had brought Daniel into favour and tender love with the prince of the eunuchs. And the prince of the eunuchs said unto Daniel, I fear my lord the king, who hath appointed your meat and your drink: for why should he see your faces worse liking than the children which are of your sort? then shall ye make me endanger my head to the king. Then said Daniel to Melzar, whom the prince of the eunuchs had set over Daniel, Hananiah, Mishael, and Azariah, Prove thy servants, I beseech thee, ten days; and let them give us pulse to eat, and water to drink. Then let our countenances be looked upon before thee, and the countenance of the children that eat of the portion of the king's meat: and as thou seest, deal with thy servants. So he consented to them in this matter, and proved them ten days. And at the end of ten days their countenances appeared fairer and fatter in flesh than all the children which did eat the portion of the king's meat.

Daniel 1:9-15

The prince of the eunuchs could have been killed for disobeying the king's order to feed these men, so the prince refused. But Daniel didn't give up. Instead, he asked the man who served their food to consent to a ten-day experiment. It says a lot about Daniel's character and reputation that this prince of the eunuchs was willing to set aside his orders for ten days. It also says a lot about God that, after ten days, Daniel and his friends "appeared fairer and fatter" than all the rest of the king's candidates.

Many people have taken this portion of Scripture as validation for the superiority of the vegetarian diet. But we can't assume from these verses that Daniel never ate meat again. There is no indication in Scripture that once Daniel had a position in the king's government that he continued refusing to eat meat. Daniel 2 and 6 both mention Daniel's personal home. Within his own house, Daniel could have easily made his own meals in accordance with Jewish law. We can't assume that Daniel ate a vegetarian diet for the remaining sixty-plus years he was in Babylon, but neither should we assume he did not. Daniel's diet was not the reason he excelled. Vegetarianism is not what these verses are talking about.

First Samuel says that God honors those who honor Him (1 Sam. 2:30). Daniel, Hananiah (Shadrach), Mishael (Meshach), and Azariah (Abednego) honored God by obeying His Word instead of the king's. You see, the Babylonians didn't follow Jewish dietary laws. They ate unclean meats like pork and shellfish (Lev. 11:7-8 and 10-11). They sacrificed their meats to idols, and since they butchered animals by strangulation, they ate their meat with the lifeblood still in it (Gen. 9:4). Essentially, King Nebuchadnezzar's table was not kosher. This was the issue.

These verses in Daniel are not indications of the diets New Testament believers should observe. In Genesis, God told Noah, "Every moving thing that liveth shall be meat for you; even as the green herb have I given you all things" (Gen. 9:3). First Timothy clearly says that "commanding to abstain from meats" is a doctrine of the devil (1 Tim. 4:1-3).

And commanding to abstain from meats, which God hath created to be received with thanksgiving of them which believe and know the truth. For every creature of God is good, and nothing to be refused, if it be received with thanksgiving. For it is sanctified by the word of God and prayer.

1 Timothy 4:3-5

I don't believe there is anything wrong with a person choosing not to eat meat. But "commanding to abstain," or preaching that doing so makes a person holier or that they have to eat this way in order to minister, is a doctrine of devils. There were dietary laws in the Old Testament that forbade the eating of shellfish and pork and rabbits and a whole host of things. There were laws regulating how a person could prepare their food and even when certain foods could be eaten. But because of the cross, those regulations have been removed. Under the New Covenant, there is nothing wrong with eating pork. There is nothing wrong with having cheese on your hamburger. Nothing is to be refused if it is received with thanksgiving (1 Tim.4:4).

Now, this doesn't mean you can get out of balance and just eat anything you want. You need to use wisdom. Eating half a chocolate cake for supper and topping it off with a quart of ice cream is going to make your body rebel. There will be consequences—some more immediate than others. But the kingdom of God is not about "meat and drink;" it's about being right with God (Rom. 14:17).

Daniel's diet didn't make him superior to the other men around King Nebuchadnezzar; it was his relationship with God that made the difference. Daniel 1 makes it very clear that God was the one who gave Daniel and his friends their abilities.

As for these four children, God gave them knowledge and skill in all learning and wisdom: and Daniel had understanding in all visions and dreams. Now at the end of the days that the king had said he should bring them in, then the prince of the eunuchs brought them in before Nebuchadnezzar. And the king communed with them; and among them all was found none like Daniel, Hananiah, Mishael, and Azariah: therefore stood they before the king. And in all matters of wisdom and understanding, that the king enquired of them, he found them ten times better than all the magicians and astrologers that were in all his realm.

Daniel 1:17-20

A personal relationship with God was foundational to the success of each of these men in Babylon. Relationship not only protected them from evil, but it also opened the door to wisdom and favor unmatched by their peers. Daniel 1:20 says that God gave Daniel and his friends wisdom and understanding ten times better than the wisdom of their peers! Only God can do that. And only a relationship with God can open that door.

Chapter Seven

It's Limitless

A s I said before, you are more than what you can see or feel. You are a spirit, created in the image of God. The things you see and feel are temporary. They are limited by time and space. But God is eternal; He is not limited by time or contained by space. And your spirit has been remade *exactly* like His (Rom. 8:9-11). It is limitless! However, dependence on your natural talents and abilities—whether you have many or few—will impose limits on what God can do.

> *Yea, they turned back and tempted God, and limited the Holy One of Israel. They remembered not his hand, nor the day when he delivered them from the enemy.*

> **Psalm 78:41-42**

You know the story of the Israelites in Egypt. Two hundred years after Joseph died, a new Pharaoh came into power. This Pharaoh had not heard of Joseph and when he saw the numbers of the Israelites growing, he feared what they might be able to do if united with his enemies. So he forced them into slavery. But God saw the Israelites' mistreatment, heard their cries, and sent a deliverer (Ex. 1-3). After an amazing display of God's power, the Israelites left Egypt a free people, laden with a conqueror's treasure (Ex. 7-14). But shortly after the sounds of victory faded, the people began to complain. They did not remember the Lord's hand; they did not remember His faithfulness or His power (Ps. 78:42), and this limited what He could do in their lives.

Don't limit God in your life. Don't limit what He can accomplish through you. Recognize who you are in the spirit—the things God has done in you through Christ (Eph. 2:1-10). Remember God's faithfulness. Remember His hand and learn to depend on His grace (Heb. 13:21).

When I pastored in Childress, Texas, Jamie and I rented a house with a large addition on the back. The house itself was really small, but the addition could hold around 150 people. So we used that room for our church services. Well, the man I was renting the house from decided to sell. Since we would have lost the place where our church met and we didn't have enough money to buy a separate building, we decided to buy that house. Thankfully, the owner agreed to carry the note for us, but not long afterward, we ran out of money. As soon as I knew we weren't going to be able to make that month's house payment, I approached the owner.

"I'm sorry," I said. "I don't have the money today, but I am going to get it. I will *never* not pay my bills."

The man appreciated my honesty and my refusal to ignore the issue, so he offered to let me work off my debt in his photography studio. But I was pastoring a church and wasn't looking for a job—and I knew nothing about photography! Still, I felt obligated to do what I could to pay my debt (and I was pretty sure the owner would view the standard Christian response of "I'm trusting God" as just an excuse.) So, I went to work.

During my first day on the job, the man gave me the task of developing school pictures for the local high school. He had already taken all the headshots, but his developer had quit. That left the man trying to develop pictures, run the studio, and do sittings for new clients all at the same time. He was falling behind. When I came on-board, the school project deadline had already passed. The school was one of this man's biggest clients, and he was looking at the distinct possibility of losing the business.

I had zero experience developing pictures, but the boss was desperate. Trying to explain how the photography process worked, he shot a picture, developed it, and took me outside.

"What's wrong with this picture?" he asked.

"Nothing," I said. "It looks great."

"There's too much magenta," he responded.

At first I thought, *What in the world is magenta?* But as my boss began to teach me about developing, I realized that not knowing about magenta was the least of my shortcomings. No matter how many times he told me what to do, I just couldn't get it.

51

I prayed, "God, if I am going to work this job, I'm going to be the best employee this guy's ever had. Teach me what to do." Then I started praying in tongues, and God showed me what to do.

One day after I had laid out a set of pictures to dry, my boss came in. "Look at this," he exclaimed. "This is beautiful! How did you do this? I've been developing pictures for over twenty-five years, and I've only been able to do this once!" I showed him the rest of the pictures I'd been working on—and they all looked exactly the same. "I don't know how you're doing this," he continued, "but keep doing it."

The process God showed me, though advanced, was saving time and paper. Within a couple of months, I helped bring this man's business out of bankruptcy. He was so thrilled that he offered to make me a partner, splitting the business fifty-fifty.

Of course, I refused, because God had called me to minister. But before I left the business, I had to train my replacement. I did exactly as my boss had done. I took a picture, developed it, and walked the new trainee out into the sunlight. "What's wrong with this picture?" I asked.

"Nothing," he replied. "It looks fine."

"Too much magenta," I said. (I'd been waiting forever to say that!) I went on to explain the development process to this new recruit, but he kept interrupting.

"How do you know where to set this?" he would ask.

"How do you know how much color to add here?" he'd mumble.

"How do you … how do you … how do you …?"

I finally threw my hands up and said, "I don't know! All I do is pray in tongues, and God gives me wisdom."

"Then how am I supposed to do it?" he asked with a look of panic on his face.

"I can lead you in the baptism of the Holy Spirit," I said. "I can teach you how to pray in tongues, but I can't teach you how to develop these pictures. You're on your own."

Developing pictures was beyond my natural abilities. I didn't know what I was doing, but I did know Philippians 4:13: "I can do all things through Christ which strengtheneth me." Because I knew my identity in Christ, because I knew my spirit was limitless, I was able to draw on abilities far beyond my natural experience.

You see, it's impossible to fulfill your potential in Christ when you don't know who you are. I once heard a story about a man who caught a baby elephant. To keep the elephant from running away, the owner tied its foot to a large tree with a heavy chain. At first, the elephant struggled against the chain, but it was still a baby and wasn't strong enough to free itself. For days, the baby elephant tried to escape and return to its herd. It jerked. It pulled. But it couldn't free itself. Eventually, the baby elephant stopped fighting.

The owner fed the elephant and cared for it, but he never took off the chain. As the elephant grew, it became stronger. The owner was getting concerned. It seemed as if his elephant's chain was shrinking. How would he keep a full-grown elephant from breaking the chain and running away? Should he find a bigger chain? Should he find a bigger tree? As the weeks turned into months, the owner realized he didn't need to do anything. The elephant never tried to escape. Though the chain around its foot was no match for its strength now, the elephant was "convinced" that it couldn't escape, so it didn't try.

People are like that. They tie themselves to bad decisions. They tie themselves to past failures. And because they only know themselves in the natural, they limit what they can do. They limit what God can do through them. One of the first steps in having an excellent spirit is to break those chains. Find out who you are in Christ. Make your relationship with God personal. Stop being held by the imaginary chains of your past. In Christ, your chains are gone (Gal. 5:1). You are limitless!

Chapter Eight

It's Not About You

Your relationship with God may be personal, but it's not about you. Everything we are, everything good we have, comes from God (1 Cor. 4:7; James 1:17). Our life, our health, our talents, our opportunities, even our faith—it all comes from God (Rom. 12:3 and 6-8). A person with an excellent spirit recognizes that.

Because of their excellence, Daniel, Hananiah, Mishael, and Azariah were promoted to positions of leadership before the end of the first chapter of the book of Daniel. People in these types of leadership positions were honored. They were sought out. They were submitted to and even bowed before. For men as young as Daniel and his friends, it would have been easy to become prideful. But they didn't.

In Daniel 2, King Nebuchadnezzar had a dream. His dream was so disturbing that he called for all the astrologers and magicians of his kingdom to try to interpret it. "I know this dream is important," he said, "but I can't remember it. You tell me the dream and what it means." Of course, none of his men could tell him the dream, much less its meaning. They said, "We can't do that. No king, no matter how great, has ever asked such a thing. What you ask is too hard; only a god could answer you." The king was so angry at their response that he gave the order for all of his wise men to be put to death—even those not at the meeting.

Palace guards immediately went in search of all the king's wise men, which would have included Daniel, Hananiah, Mishael, and Azariah. When Daniel was found, he asked Arioch, the commander of the guards, what had happened to cause such a hasty act from the king. Arioch explained what happened, and Daniel immediately went before King Nebuchadnezzar. He said, "Don't worry, king. Give me some time and I will tell you your dream. Tomorrow I will bring its interpretation."

Because Daniel and his friends had already found favor in the eyes of the king, Nebuchadnezzar granted Daniel's request. (Remember in chapter 1, the king had found the Jewish men to be ten times wiser than any other men in his kingdom. That favor was working for them here.) Daniel returned to his house and asked his friends, Hananiah, Mishael, and Azariah, to pray for him. Then he went to sleep.

It amazes me that Daniel was able to sleep the night before he was supposed to be killed! The order had gone out to kill all the wise men of the kingdom. If Daniel didn't make good on his promise to the king, he and his friends would be killed the next morning. Yet he slept. Most Christians facing a life or death situation like this would have been up all night praying, but Daniel went to sleep. Without confidence in God, that would have been impossible. And while Daniel slept, God gave him a dream. The next day, Daniel went before King Nebuchadnezzar knowing both the king's dream and its interpretation.

The king answered and said to Daniel, whose name was Belteshazzar, Art thou able to make known unto me the dream which I have seen, and the interpretation thereof? Daniel answered in the presence of the king, and said, The secret which the king hath demanded cannot the wise men, the astrologers, the magicians, the soothsayers, shew unto the king; But there is a God in heaven that revealeth secrets, and maketh known to the king Nebuchadnezzar what shall be in the latter days. Thy dream, and the visions of thy head upon thy bed, are these; As for thee, O king, thy thoughts came into thy mind upon thy bed, what should come to pass hereafter: and he that revealeth secrets maketh known to thee what shall come to pass. But as for me, this secret is not revealed to me for any wisdom that I have more than any living, but for their sakes that shall make known the interpretation to the king, and that thou mightest know the thoughts of thy heart.

Daniel 2:26-30

Before Daniel told the king the meaning of his dream, Daniel made sure to point Nebuchadnezzar to its source. Daniel didn't take credit for understanding the king's dream. He said, "King, this interpretation is not from me; no man could know such things. My great wisdom hasn't figured this out. Only God can reveal secrets." Wow! Daniel had just been shown something no other person on the face of the earth knew, but he didn't take credit for it. He gave the glory to God.

That's humility! Humility is a characteristic of an excellent spirit. Excellence recognizes that God is the source of all blessings. He is the One who gives life. He is the One who gives talents, abilities, creativity, and strength.

First Corinthians 4:7 says:

> *For who maketh thee to differ from another? and what hast thou that thou didst not receive? now if thou didst receive it, why dost thou glory, as if thou hadst not received it?*

What great logic! What makes you different or better than anyone else? What do you have that you haven't received? All your talents and abilities come from God. If you can draw or work with wood, God gave you that talent. If you can talk to people and sell things, God gave you that ability. If you have a mind for numbers and accounting, it comes from God.

A few years ago, I heard Keith Moore give a great example of this concept. He said that his ability to speak to crowds had always been a part of him. Even as a child, he loved making presentations and talking with others. Public speaking had always been easy for him. He could give speeches without feeling nervous.

As he grew up, he thought this ability was just something normal, something inborn that would always be a part of him. But Keith didn't want to take any of God's gifts for granted, so one day he prayed and asked God to show him the truth of James 1:17—that every good and perfect gift comes from God.

The morning after that prayer, Keith woke up and went to teach at Rhema Healing School as usual. He said that he taught at healing school regularly and never bothered to prepare because he had such a revelation of healing that every time he got up, the words would just flow out of his spirit. But not that morning. That morning, he couldn't remember scriptures. He struggled to put two words together. He couldn't think of anything to say.

He decided to start the song service, but he couldn't think of any songs either. When someone requested a song, he couldn't remember the words or what notes went together to make the appropriate chords. He said that for three days, he struggled to accomplish anything. Then just as suddenly as his abilities left, they all came back. At this point, Keith realized that everything he had—even the abilities he'd had his whole life and taken for granted—was from God.

I've never had natural abilities like Keith, so I've never struggled with thinking that my accomplishments were really my own. Everything I'm doing today is completely contrary to my natural tendencies. Growing up, I was an introvert. The thought of standing in front of people or speaking to more than one or two of them at a time petrified me. Yet now I speak to millions every day. I know that this ability is a gift from God, and that keeps me humble.

Humility recognizes God. Humility isn't thinking badly of yourself, but neither is it ignoring the good things in your life. True humility isn't about you. Pride, on the other hand, is all about you. Humility recognizes the good things God has done in your life and gives Him the credit for them. That's what Daniel did. When he went to the king, Daniel said, "Here's the interpretation, king. But I want you to know that my great wisdom didn't figure this out. This came from God."

Humility never takes credit for what it didn't do. It recognizes God. Daniel didn't give himself wisdom. He didn't create his mind. God did. In himself, Daniel couldn't understand the meaning of the king's dream—he didn't even know what the dream was! Only God could reveal it to him. You see, Daniel had a personal relationship with God, and that relationship opened the door to blessings and abilities beyond his wildest imagination. Daniel knew those blessings weren't about him. He didn't earn them. He didn't deserve them. But God, out of His great love, gave them to him anyway.

Chapter Nine

True Humility Is God-Dependent

Humility is a huge part of an excellent spirit. But over the years, I've noticed that not many people understand what true humility is. Romans 12:3 tells us not to think more highly of ourselves than we ought, but it doesn't say that we should think lower of ourselves, either. God doesn't make junk, so to be constantly berating ourselves or hiding the good things God has given us is wrong. When we do that, we are actually stealing His praise.

I am the LORD: that is my name: and my glory will I not give to another, neither my praise to graven images.

Isaiah 42:8

For mine own sake, even for mine own sake, will I do it: for how should my name be polluted? and I will not give my glory unto another.

Isaiah 48:11

God will not share His glory with another. Neither will He tolerate us "polluting" His name through a false sense of humility. We need to think of ourselves soberly, yet righteously. If you are taking credit for a God-given talent or ability, you aren't being humble and you're limiting how God can promote you. Similarly, if you're constantly brushing aside God's protection and blessing as coincidence or nothing special, you are not operating in humility. True humility recognizes God.

When we tape television programs, my staff typically sits me down and shoots two weeks' worth of programming in one day. I usually have a topic I want to cover, but I don't plan everything out; I just sit down and share out of my heart. (I actually get the easy job. All I have to do is start talking—my staff does everything else to make it look and sound good.)

I've had guests sit in and watch the way I minister during these tapings who later stop me in awe. They just can't believe I don't come to the table "more prepared." I tell them, "I've spent years seeking God and meditating on these scriptures. These things are in my heart. The ability to pull them out when I need them comes from God. It's His anointing to do what He has called me to do—and that is to teach."

I'm not bragging when I say these things. Why would I boast about my abilities? I have nothing that I have not received from God. When I say these things, I'm acknowledging the good that

God has done in and through me. I'm giving Him credit. I'm being humble.

Brothers and sisters, you can't walk in excellence without humility. This may be hard to hear, especially for those who have worked their whole lives to become self-sufficient, but humility is not self-sufficiency. It is not self-confidence. Humility is being God-confident. It's being God-dependent. Humility says, "There is a God, and I'm not Him!"

Self-confidence or self-sufficiency is pride. Independence from God is pride. And God does not promote pride.

But he giveth more grace. Wherefore he saith, God resisteth the proud, but giveth grace unto the humble.

James 4:6

God resists pride. The word *resist* means to "actively fight against." God actively fights against pride. Under the New Covenant, God is not at war with you. He does not fight against you personally. But He does fight against pride. God will not promote pride.

Jesus, the Son of God and God's perfect representative (Heb. 1:2-3), said, "I am meek and lowly in heart" (Matt. 11:29). God is a meek God. He is a humble God. Jesus never promoted Himself. But neither did He deny who He was. He told people, "I am the way, the truth, and the life" (John 14:6), but He also said that He could do nothing of Himself but only what He saw His Father doing (John 5:19). Jesus wasn't inflated with pride; He spoke the truth while giving credit to His Father. That's God-dependence. That's humility.

Religion has presented a warped definition of humility. It has skewed humility to mean low self-esteem. Religion has taught that debasing oneself is humility. But that can actually be pride.

In the church I attended while growing up, I remember a person who often got up to sing a special. He would say, "Well, the Lord said to make a joyful noise, so that's what I'm going to do. I'm not a great singer, but I'm going to make a joyful noise." Then he would belt out an operatic song he'd spent weeks preparing. Boy could he sing! I found out later that he'd had voice lessons. His words didn't mean anything. He wasn't really humble. It was just a religious con. This person was putting himself down in the hopes that someone else would compliment him and say, "That was awesome. What a beautiful voice." If someone actually told him, "You were right; you can't sing," I'm sure he wouldn't have accepted that type of remark as graciously.

People can get very proud of their "humility." But true humility is not this idea of *I am nothing; I can do nothing.* True humility doesn't exalt self. True humility doesn't debase self. True humility isn't about self at all. Self is pride. Highlighting your accomplishments is pride. The need to share your opinion is pride. Slandering or gossiping about someone to improve your reputation is pride. Avoiding criticism is pride. Worrying about what other people think is pride.

True humility doesn't have an opinion one way or the other. True humility just says what is true. Numbers 12:3 says that "Moses was very meek, above all the men which were upon the face of the earth." This might not seem that important a statement, but Moses is the one who wrote that! Under the inspiration of the Holy Spirit, he said, "I am the meekest man on the face of the whole earth." According to religion's definition of humility, that statement would have disqualified Moses from being considered truly humble.

I once heard a story about a church that wanted to honor humility. They decided to bring the most humble man in their congregation to the front of the church and present him with a special prize. To determine who was the meekest member of their church, they took a vote. It was nearly a unanimous decision. So, the next Sunday, they brought "dear old brother so-and-so" to the front of the sanctuary and presented him with a large "Humble" button. "Dear old brother so-and-so" accepted their button with thanks, and everyone was shocked because they felt that a truly humble person would never have accepted a button that advertised their strengths or abilities. They thought that "dear old brother so-and-so" couldn't have been truly humble, so they ended up taking his button away. But their perspective was wrong. "Dear old brother so-and-so" hadn't declared himself the most humble. The church had—by a nearly unanimous vote!

True humily is saying about yourself what God says about you. True humility agrees with God. If God says you are the meekest person on the planet, it would be pride for you to disagree with that. If God says you are the righteousness of God in Christ (2 Cor. 5:21), then you are. To say otherwise would be exalting your own opinion above God's opinion.

Good things happen when we stop and acknowledge what God has done in our lives. Philemon 6 says that thankfulness—acknowledging what God has done—makes our faith effective. We need to know it is "Christ in [us], the hope of glory" (Col. 1:27, brackets added). We need to know that we can "do all things through Christ" (Phil. 4:13). But we have to keep that in balance with the truth that "without [Christ we] can do nothing" (John 15:5, brackets added).

I live in the mountains, and the road to my house is a dirt road with drainage ditches on both sides. I can't swerve on that road to avoid wandering rabbits and squirrels without ending up in one of those ditches. I have to stay in the middle of the road. The Word of God is like that road. It contains verses and concepts that appear to contradict themselves. These apparent contradictions are like ditches that, if taken alone, will derail a person's life. (By the way, God's Word never contradicts itself; taken as a whole, the Word actually complements and agrees with itself.) We have to stay balanced in the Word of God, just like I have to stay in the middle of my dirt road to make it home.

I can't take a verse like Philippians 4:13, "I can do all things through Christ," and become arrogant in my successes, thinking I don't need God. Neither can I take a verse like John 15:5, "without [Christ I] can do nothing" (brackets added), and constantly live in a state of indecision. While it is true that I can't do anything without Christ, it is also true that I am never without Christ (Heb. 13:5). To stay out of the ditch, I have to stay balanced. I have to maintain a holy dissatisfaction with myself and my own abilities, while nurturing great satisfaction and contentment with who I am in Christ Jesus.

Humility knows that every good thing is a result of the grace of God. Without the grace of God—without His supernatural ability and empowerment—we can do nothing. The grace of God gave us Christ. It gave us the opportunity to have a relationship with God apart from the rules and regulations of the

Law. However, when some people hear about the grace of God, they get so excited about not having to be perfect that they begin leading self-indulgent lives. These people have taken one concept from the Word out of context and have swerved into a ditch of error.

While it is true that grace has released us from the fear of punishment, grace also teaches us to "live soberly, righteously, and godly" in the midst of a self-indulgent society (Titus 2:12). Grace teaches us to be humble and to recognize that our position is only ours through Christ. This is the difference between an excellent spirit and one of perfectionism.

The *Houghton Mifflin American Heritage Electronic Dictionary* defines perfectionism as "a tendency to set extremely high standards and to be dissatisfied with anything less" (s.v. "perfectionism"). Perfectionism is proud and arrogant. It is critical and judgmental of people, ideas, and work that doesn't meet its standard. But an excellent spirit is humble. Excellence still has high standards, but it recognizes the roles that others—especially God—play in meeting those standards. True humility doesn't deny what God has done. True humility just denies that "self" had anything to do with it!

Chapter Ten

The Power of Obedience

Humility requires submission. It recognizes authority and yields to that authority. Those who know that the Word says to love their neighbor (Mark 12:33) and to give as God has prospered them (1 Cor. 16:2) but then rely on God's grace to disobey the Word are fooling themselves. James said to be "doers of the word, and not hearers only" (James 1:22). People who refuse to "do" the Word because they are living under grace are not people of humility. They have not submitted themselves to God. They are prideful. They have exalted their own ideas above God's and have placed themselves on the throne of their own lives.

*Though the L*ORD *be high, yet hath he respect unto the lowly: but the proud he knoweth afar off.*

Psalm 138:6

God cannot get close to pride. That doesn't mean He doesn't love prideful people or that He punishes or rejects those who are prideful. It just means that He can't bless pride. James also said, "God resisteth the proud" (James 4:6), "Submit yourselves therefore to God" (James 4:7), and "Draw nigh to God, and he will draw nigh to you" (James 4:8). How do you "draw nigh" to God? Based on this context, you draw nigh to God by submitting to Him, by choosing humility.

Intimacy with God requires humility. You can't draw nigh to God if you are proud, self-centered, and doing your own thing. God still loves you, and He'll deal with you based on your covenant with Him based on grace. He won't give you the punishment you deserve; but if you really want intimacy with God, you have to humble yourself and acknowledge Him as God.

Often when people are in trouble, they spend time in prayer and in the Word, but when everything is going well, they forget their relationship with God. Most people only humble themselves—they only depend on God—when things are beyond their control, when they don't have any other option. That's pride.

A person who is humble depends on God all the time. One of the ways humility shows its dependence is through obedience. When God commands something, a person of humility will do it. For instance, when God told me to start Charis Bible College, I obeyed. I didn't even like Bible colleges! It has been over twenty years since we started Charis and it's still changing lives all over the world today. People are streaming into Charis as fast as we can accommodate them! Yet I'm still amazed at the number of people interested in attending Charis Colorado who say things like, "I believe God wants me to come, but…" and then they list a bunch of reasons why they can't come. Once a guy even told me, "But I live under a bridge."

"We've got bridges in Colorado," I said.

Other people have said things like, "But I have dogs," to which I respond, "They allow dogs in Colorado."

One man from Chicago said, "I know beyond a shadow of a doubt that God told me to come to Charis, but I'm engaged. My fiancée told me she'd break off our engagement if I came. My parents don't even support my desire to come. They talked to our pastor, and he said you were a cult. Now they're threatening to disinherit me if I come. What should I do?"

"If God told you to come," I said to him, "then come."

"But what about…?"

"Don't worry about that," I interrupted. "Just obey God."

Proverbs 3:5-7 says:

Trust in the LORD with all thine heart; and lean not unto thine own understanding. In all thy ways acknowledge him, and he shall direct thy paths. Be not wise in thine own eyes: fear the LORD, and depart from evil.

Don't be "wise in your own eyes." Trust God. Acknowledge Him and He will direct your path. That's humility. Don't try to figure out all the things that might happen before you obey

God. That's not God-dependence; that's pride. That's trusting in yourself.

When God told Abraham to leave his father's house and all of his brethren (Acts 7:2-3), Abraham did not obey. Instead, he left Ur with his father and nephew and dwelt in Haran (Gen. 11:31). Then after his father's death (Gen. 11:32), Abraham entered into Canaan with his wife, his nephew Lot, and all the people they had acquired in Haran (Gen. 12:1-5).

I'm sure Abraham was thinking that since his brother, Lot's father, had died, it was his responsibility to help Lot. But God told Abraham to leave his father's house and *all* of his brethren. Most people probably think Abraham's actions were commendable, but Abraham didn't do what God told him to do. And look at the consequences.

Eventually Abraham's and Lot's possessions grew so numerous that the land they traveled could not support them both. Fights began breaking out between their herdsmen, until they were forced to separate. Lot moved into the land of Sodom, and Abraham moved further into Canaan. When Abraham finally obeyed God (leaving *all* of his brethren), God was able to bless him. God promised, "For all the land which thou seest, to thee will I give it, and to thy seed for ever. And I will make thy seed as the dust of the earth" (Gen. 13:15-16).

It took years for Abraham to get to the place where God could bless him because he only partially obeyed God. Since Abraham leaned on his own understanding and trusted his own wisdom, Lot suffered. After Lot moved to Sodom, he was kidnapped in a border dispute, lost two of his daughters (and their husbands) to the perversion of Sodom, was forced to leave his home, saw Sodom and Gomorrah destroyed, witnessed his wife turn into a pillar of salt, and was party to his remaining daughters committing incest with him and starting the family line of two of Israel's mortal enemies (Gen. 14 and 19). I'm not sure how it could have been much worse if Lot had stayed in Haran!

My point is this: When we lean on our own understanding, we mess things up. We're *always, always, always* better off obeying God! Whatever your logic is for not obeying God, it is not good enough. Humility obeys God. It doesn't argue. It doesn't make excuses. It just obeys.

Since my experience with the Lord on March 23, 1968, when I made an unconditional, absolute surrender to God to the best of my ability, I have made it a point to obey Him. Every time God has spoken to me, even when it didn't look like what He said would work out to my benefit, I have obeyed. I'm not saying I've done it perfectly, but as soon as I figure out what the Lord wants, that's what I do.

For example, when God directed me to quit school, I obeyed, even though I knew I would lose my student deferment. Then I was drafted and sent to Vietnam where I literally faced death. But during that time, I also grew in the Word and received a revelation that has been foundational in my walk with God and in my ministry. When God told me to go into the ministry, I did. I burned all my bridges. I lost family and friends and endured criticism. But I obeyed. When God told me to go to Pritchett, Colorado—a place with only 144 people that looked like the death of my vision—I obeyed. I followed God in these little steps and my humility, my dependence on Him, promoted me to where I am today.

I don't think most people realize what they're doing when they wrestle with obeying God. In a sense, debating about whether or not to obey is actually questioning God. It's thinking that God didn't realize all He was asking of you, that He didn't consider the consequences. It is thinking you know more than God, that your wisdom is greater than His. That's pride!

Scripture says, "The way of man is not in himself: it is not in man that walketh to direct his steps" (Jer. 10:23). We are not smart enough to run our own lives. We need God. But God always gives us a choice. He won't force us to submit to Him. He won't force us to obey.

Jesus told us to deny ourselves, take up our cross, and follow Him (Matt. 16:24). Denying self is humility. Denying your own wisdom and logic and just going by what God says—that's humility. And that's an excellent spirit!

Chapter Eleven

Don't Compromise

An excellent spirit or attitude is the key to promotion. Yet many people think that as long as they *do* the right thing, they will succeed. They think that going through the motions of success will bring success. But that's not true. Wrong attitude voids right actions.

First Corinthians 13:1-3 says:

Though I speak with the tongues of men and of angels, and have not charity, I am become as sounding brass, or a tinkling cymbal. And though I have the gift of prophecy, and understand all mysteries, and all knowledge; and though I have all faith, so that I could remove mountains, and have not charity, I am nothing. And though I bestow all my goods to feed the poor, and though I give my body to be burned, and have not charity, it profiteth me nothing.

Speaking in tongues, using your faith, and giving to the poor are all good things. But doing "good things" without the right motivation—without God's kind of love—is worthless. It profits nothing. The above passage echoes what Jesus said about hypocrites who love to fast and pray and give to be seen by people (Matt. 6:1-18). God cannot reward them. He cannot bless them. Jesus said they already have their reward.

Mimicking the actions of biblical heroes like Daniel, Joseph, and Paul without the heart that produced those actions leads to frustration, and ultimately failure. That's because in God's kingdom, the attitude behind a person's action is more important than the action itself (Prov. 21:2).

A person with right motivation is a person of integrity. Integrity does what's right when everyone is watching, as well as when no one is watching. Integrity is consistent. It does not compromise.

Compromise is a big problem in today's society. People don't have strong convictions about anything. They can't handle persecution. They don't know how to deal with conflict, so they compromise to keep from rocking the boat. Even driving down the road, I see evidence of this compromise. Bumper stickers with "coexist" written out in different religious symbols are everywhere. But the idea that there are many ways to God is completely contrary to what the Bible teaches. There aren't many different ways to God. There is only one way—Jesus Christ (John 14:6).

Compromise is the language of the devil. Whatever you compromise to get or to keep—including "peace"—you'll eventually lose. But God honors conviction. I could take you through the

Bible, from Genesis to Maps, and show you person after person whom God honored for having firm conviction and for refusing to compromise. One of those examples is Daniel. Others are his friends Hananiah, Mishael, and Azariah. After Daniel interpreted the king's dream, he was promoted and made "ruler over the whole province of Babylon" (Dan. 2:48). Hananiah, Mishael, and Azariah were promoted as well.

After a while, Nebuchadnezzar decided to make his dream of a statue with a head of gold a reality by creating a huge statue of himself. The image he commissioned was made of gold. It stood ninety feet high and nine feet wide. When it was complete, Nebuchadnezzar called together all the rulers, princes, presidents, and leaders of his kingdom to worship his image.

Then an herald cried aloud, To you it is commanded, O people, nations, and languages, That at what time ye hear the sound of the cornet, flute, harp, sackbut, psaltery, dulcimer, and all kinds of musick, ye fall down and worship the golden image that Nebuchadnezzar the king hath set up: And whoso falleth not down and worshippeth shall the same hour be cast into the midst of a burning fiery furnace. Therefore at that time, when all the people heard the sound of the cornet, flute, harp, sackbut, psaltery, and all kinds of musick, all the people, the nations, and the languages, fell down and worshipped the golden image that Nebuchadnezzar the king had set up.

Daniel 3:4-7

But three men refused. Hananiah, Mishael, and Azariah, whom the Babylonians had renamed Shadrach, Meshach, and Abednego, literally stood up to the king. They refused to bow.

77

They refused to compromise. When Nebuchadnezzar heard of their civil disobedience, he was furious.

> *Wherefore at that time certain Chaldeans came near, and accused the Jews.... There are certain Jews whom thou hast set over the affairs of the province of Babylon, Shadrach, Meshach, and Abednego; these men, O king, have not regarded thee: they serve not thy gods, nor worship the golden image which thou hast set up. Then Nebuchadnezzar in his rage and fury commanded to bring Shadrach, Meshach, and Abednego. Then they brought these men before the king.*

Daniel 3:8 and 12-13

Now remember, Nebuchadnezzar was the strongest, most powerful man on the face of the earth at this time. He had conquered the whole of the known world. Yet Shadrach, Meshach, and Abednego weren't afraid. Even when the king singled them out and commanded that they bow before his image or die, these faithful men refused. They said:

> *O Nebuchadnezzar, we are not careful to answer thee in this matter. If it be so, our God whom we serve is able to deliver us from the burning fiery furnace, and he will deliver us out of thine hand, O king. But if not, be it known unto thee, O king, that we will not serve thy gods, nor worship the golden image which thou hast set up.*

Daniel 3:16-18

Man, that is amazing! These men not only did the right thing by refusing to bow, but they also told the king in no uncertain terms, "We're not worried. Your threats are not a big deal. We aren't afraid of what you can do to us." What an attitude! These men weren't "careful." They didn't think about the consequences. They just obeyed God and refused to compromise their convictions (Ex. 20:3-5).

The average person could never do that. The average person is too afraid of man. Proverbs 29:25 says, "The fear of man bringeth a snare." If you're afraid of man, you will fall into a snare. You'll always compromise and feel pressured and criticized. But when God is your source, when He is your ultimate authority, you understand the psalmist's declaration that "The LORD is on my side; I will not fear: what can man do unto me?" (Ps. 118:6).

Many years ago, God gave me a prophecy. I was walking through a time of intense criticism and struggling with fear of man. It felt like everyone was against me and that I was standing alone. I couldn't seem to get past it. Then one night, a man called me out during a meeting and said, "I see you on a racetrack. You're out in front; you're leading the way. But the crowd is yelling at you. They're telling you that you're doing everything wrong. And I see you getting off the track and going into the stands to argue with the spectators." Then this man said, "Even if you win the argument, you're going to lose the race. Forget the people. Stay on track." Has that ever been a word from God for me!

I believe that is a word from God for you, too. Be a person of excellence. Stay out of the stands. Even if you win the argument, you're going to lose the race. Don't let Satan distract you with the fear of man. Don't depend on others' opinions. That is the wrong place to base your happiness. Do what God tells you to do. Don't compromise. Don't let potential problems or potential loss sidetrack you. Shadrach, Meshach, and Abednego didn't, and here we are still talking about them 3,000 years later!

Chapter Twelve

An Eternal Perspective

As believers, we've got to stop worrying about what other people think. We have to stop living to please man. Jesus was not a man-pleaser. When He was teaching in a synagogue in Capernaum, Jesus said, "I am the bread of life. Whoever eats of Me will live forever" (John 6:51, paraphrase mine). When Jesus said this, the Jews missed the spiritual significance of His statement. They thought He was talking about cannibalism. But Jesus didn't apologize for the misunderstanding. He didn't try to explain Himself. He actually made it worse by saying, "Except ye eat the flesh of the Son of man, and drink his blood, ye have no life in you" (John 6:53). Jesus wasn't worried about pleasing man. He wanted to please His Father.

When the people following Jesus heard about His new teaching, they began grumbling. Jesus asked, "Doth this offend you?" (John 6:61). Again, we see Him completely unmoved by man's opinions. Jesus continued, "I'm not surprised that some of you don't believe. No man can come to Me without God's help" (John 6:64-65, paraphrase mine). At this, many of His disciples left!

But Jesus still refused to compromise. Instead, He turned to the Twelve and asked, "Will ye also go away?" (John 6:67), meaning, "There's the door. Are you guys committed, or do you want to leave too?"

Sadly, most ministers today are so afraid of losing a following or saying something that might cause criticism that they compromise the truth. I heard about a Barna survey that asked a group of pastors if they believed the Word of God had an answer for every current social issue we face, and 90 percent of respondents said "Yes." The next survey question asked each pastor if they taught on what the Bible says about these social issues, and only 10 percent responded that yes, they teach on social issues. Eighty percent of these pastors knew what the Bible had to say, but would not teach it because it wasn't popular! They were afraid the truth would cost them members or money.

Years ago the Lord gave me a word of knowledge for someone, but I didn't want to share it. I was hesitant because I knew this person wasn't going to like what I had to say. I knew they would reject it. But the Lord spoke to me and said, "Speak. You give *them* the choice to accept or reject My Word. Don't reject it for them."

When we don't tell a person the truth because we're afraid they'll reject it, we've just rejected the truth for them. That's not fair. God has given the whole world the chance to accept or reject truth for themselves. Who are we to take that opportunity away? We need to love people enough to tell them the truth. Truth is what sets people free (John 8:32).

When Nebuchadnezzar confronted Shadrach, Meshach, and Abednego and told them to bow before his image, they refused. Even in the face of death, they would not compromise. And because they knew that God's authority outranked the king's, they weren't even careful. They weren't worried. They just spoke the truth.

Some people read that and think, *That's the way I am.* But those same people won't stand up when immorality is flaunted in the public square. They don't say anything when their coworkers giggle at dirty jokes or when their children celebrate "individual rights."

We live in a society where the Supreme Court had the audacity to redefine marriage, saying that marriage can be between two men or two women. Now people are trying to petition their governments for "the right" to have multiple wives or to marry and have sex with their children or pets. They're fighting for the right to teach public school children "gender fluidity." They are advocating for Satanist clubs to be allowed in schools.

We live in a society where evil is being called good and where a spirit of antichrist roams free. And the majority of Christians aren't saying anything! They're afraid of rejection. They're afraid of criticism. Christians live life with their finger in the air, constantly testing which way the wind of public opinion is blowing.

They've allowed the spirit of political correctness to bully them into backing down from God's Word. That is not the attitude of an excellent spirit.

Jesus said, "And fear not them which kill the body, but are not able to kill the soul: but rather fear him which is able to destroy both soul and body in hell" (Matt. 10:28). It is short-term thinking that exalts the fear of man over the fear of God. The thought that you could lose a friendship or go to jail is short-term thinking. The fear of being criticized or even facing death is short-term thinking. Paul said:

For our light affliction, which is but for a moment, worketh for us a far more exceeding and eternal weight of glory; While we look not at the things which are seen, but at the things which are not seen: for the things which are seen are temporal; but the things which are not seen are eternal.

2 Corinthians 4:17-18

The reason Paul could endure imprisonment, beatings, ridicule, shipwreck, poverty, death, and all of the other hardships that came his way is because he understood those things were "but for a moment." He understood they were only temporary.

The reason Shadrach, Meshach, and Abednego were able to stand strong in the face of death is because they didn't look at things the way most people do. They didn't look at only what could be seen. They had a different perspective. They looked at things in the light of eternity.

What is this life compared to eternity? What is a little suffering? A little hardship? Even if you were to be put to death for your faith, in the light of eternity, what does it matter? Would you really consider sacrificing eternity for momentary pleasure? Or momentary safety? That's short-term thinking.

I can guarantee you that many of the Babylonian rulers in Nebuchadnezzar's day knew the image they were commanded to worship wasn't God. An undertaking as large as building a ninety-foot statue could not have remained secret for long. I'm sure at least some of those men were leaders who were given the task of overseeing the statue's construction. Some could have been in charge of finding artisans, others with ordering materials and supplies. Some of those men were likely on site every day as the statue was being erected. Those men knew the statue was manmade. They knew it wasn't a "god." Yet they bowed. And for all of their temporary power and prestige, not one of those men is remembered today.

Brothers and sisters, if you're being intimidated by people—whether they are family members, business associates, or members of your church—if you're allowing other people's criticism to stop you from standing up and speaking out for what's right, you have the wrong perspective.

God created every human being to live forever. We're all going to live forever in eternity. The only question is where. People who are afraid to stand up and do what is right aren't thinking in light of eternity. Their only thoughts are for what may advance them during the next five or ten years. That's short-term thinking. Sacrificing the future, whether theirs or someone else's, for momentary ease is wrong. That's not an excellent spirit.

God promotes faithfulness. He promotes people who won't compromise, who think in light of eternity. I remember being persecuted in the early days of my ministry by a guy who told people I was of the devil. This man had never met me or listened to me in person, but he hated me. He burned my tapes and books and encouraged others to do the same. But even after I found out who this guy was, I never said anything bad about him. I just tried to keep an excellent spirit.

Four or five years later, I attended a week of special meetings. I didn't know it at the time, but this man was there too. For some reason, the speaker at this meeting called me up at every service to compliment me about something. Toward the end of the conference, the man who had hated me and burned my books came up front and in front of 500-700 people, he fell at my feet and begged my forgiveness. He grabbed my boots. He cried. He made a spectacle of himself. I didn't demand any of it. At first, I didn't even realize who the guy was! But God knew. And because I kept an excellent spirit, because I kept doing the right thing, God honored me. He promoted me.

I'm living in a situation right now where an internationally known minister is beginning to recognize and honor me. Twenty-plus years ago, this same person came out against me viciously. They said I was of the devil. They labeled my ministry a cult. But I never got upset. I kept walking in love. I sent offerings. I blessed instead of cursed. Today, this person has completely changed their tune. They regularly watch me on television. We've ministered together. They call me. They've given me their personal phone number and invited Jamie and me to their house. You'd think we've been the best of friends for years. But they have never apologized. They've never mentioned their past statements about me. I don't know exactly what has happened to change their opinion, but I do know that if I had gotten hurt and started lashing out, if I had let my "momentary trouble" change my perspective, our relationship would not be where it is today. I would not be where I am today.

Chapter Thirteen

The Surety
of the Word

Before Daniel and his friends were taken captive, they didn't know all that God would accomplish through them in Babylon. They didn't know their wisdom would direct kings. They didn't know they'd see visions. They didn't know they'd participate in miracles. Neither did they know all that would be asked of them. They didn't know they'd be reviled as slaves. They didn't know they'd be slandered or that their lives would be threatened. But Daniel and his friends didn't let what they didn't know shake their confidence in what they did know.

Daniel, Hananiah, Mishael, and Azariah knew they belonged to God. They knew they had a covenant with Him. And they knew that regardless of the circumstances they might face, God would remain faithful. He would keep His covenant.

He hath remembered his covenant for ever, the word which he commanded to a thousand generations.

Psalm 105:8

Because of their great confidence in God, Daniel and his friends weren't afraid to speak the truth. They weren't concerned with criticism. Even in the midst of difficult circumstances, they were able to hold fast the profession of their faith (Heb. 10:23).

When Shadrach, Meshach, and Abednego refused to bow to Nebuchadnezzar's image, the king threatened to throw them into the fiery furnace, and he taunted them by asking, "And who is that god that shall deliver you out of my hands?" (Dan. 3:15). But they weren't afraid. They weren't even worried. They said:

If it be so, our God whom we serve is able to deliver us from the burning fiery furnace, and he will deliver us out of thine hand, O king. But if not, be it known unto thee, O king, that we will not serve thy gods, nor worship the golden image which thou hast set up.

Daniel 3:17-18

What great faith! Unfortunately, every time I minister using these verses, people approach me and question the three Hebrew children's statement in Daniel 3:18. For some reason, people see their "but if not" statement as a negative confession. I don't think it is. I think this statement is a great profession of faith. Shadrach, Meshach, and Abednego knew that God was bigger than the circumstances they were facing. They knew He was able to deliver them, and they believed He would. "But if not," they said, "if for some reason we die in the fire, we will still believe God, and we will still serve Him."

Let me give you a modern-day example. I believe it is God's will to heal. I believe God wants all of His children to live in health, and I've seen a lot of physical proof that my belief is accurate. I've walked in supernatural health for over forty years. I've seen blind eyes and deaf ears opened. I've seen cancers healed. I've seen people come out of wheelchairs. I've seen about every kind of miracle there is. I've even seen people raised from the dead. I believe it is God's will to heal every person, every time. But I don't see every person I pray for healed.

My sister recently died battling lung cancer. I know lung cancer wasn't God's will for her life, and she knew it too. She was believing to be healed the best she knew how, yet she died. I don't understand all the ins and outs of that situation, but one thing I do know: God didn't miss it. His Word says that healing is the children's bread (Matt. 15:21-28). Even though I didn't see my sister healed, I know God's Word is still true. He is still the God who "forgiveth **all** thine iniquities; [and] healeth **all** thy diseases" (Ps. 103:3, brackets and emphasis added).

But a lot of people let circumstances dictate their theology. They don't let the Bible get in the way of what they believe. The average Christian may read that by Jesus' stripes they *were* healed (1 Pet. 2:24), but they let their God-fearing, great-aunt Alice's battle with diabetes "prove" that God doesn't always heal His people. Romans 3:4 says, "Let God be true, but every man a liar." If God's Word says He heals *all* our diseases (Ps. 103:3), then He heals *all* our diseases. If the Word says Jesus carried our griefs and purchased our healing (Isa. 53:4-5), then He carried our griefs and purchased our healing (1 Pet. 2:24), regardless of what our experience says.

Again, I don't know what the problem was in my sister's case, but I know several people who died of cancer while professing that they were believing for healing. From the outside, it looked like they were doing everything right, but after their deaths, journals surfaced that told how they'd given up hope, how they were ready to quit fighting and meet the Lord. The journals revealed that these people were just going through the motions of faith to avoid criticism. They weren't really believing. God's Word didn't fail in those situations. The people did.

I'm believing God for a long, productive life. I'm believing to be like Moses, living to be 120 years old with my eyesight "not dim, nor [my] natural force abated" (Deut. 34:7, brackets added). But even if I don't obtain that, even if something happens and I face death before I turn 120 years old, I'm still going to believe that it is God's will to heal. I'm still going to set my faith on what the Word of God says. I know if something I'm believing for doesn't come to pass, it's not God's fault. His Word is still true. He is still faithful, even if I am not.

> *If we believe not, yet he abideth faithful: he cannot deny himself.*

> **2 Timothy 2:13**

God cannot deny Himself. He cannot deny His Word (Ps. 89:34). God and His Word are one (John 1:1). If God were to deny Himself—if He were to violate His Word—the whole universe, which was built on His Word (Ps. 33:9 and Heb. 11:3), would self-destruct. Everything is held together by the integrity of God's Word (Heb. 1:3). The Word of God is something we can count on.

Heaven and earth shall pass away, but my words shall not pass away.

Matthew 24:35

God is not a man, that he should lie; neither the son of man, that he should repent: hath he said, and shall he not do it? or hath he spoken, and shall he not make it good?

Numbers 23:19

I believe Shadrach, Meshach, and Abednego understood this. They understood God's covenant with His Word. They knew God would honor His Word. For these great men of faith, seeing the Word come to pass in their lives was just an added bonus. That's what their "but if not" statement was about. They had decided that no matter what Nebuchadnezzar did, they were sticking with God. They were sticking with His Word.

Part of having an excellent spirit is making the Word of God your sure foundation. You can't build a house without a solid foundation, and you can't build a successful life apart from God's Word.

This book of the law shall not depart out of thy mouth; but thou shalt meditate therein day and night, that thou mayest observe to do according to all that is written therein: for then thou shalt make thy way prosperous, and then thou shalt have good success.

Joshua 1:8

So, what are you building your life upon?

Chapter Fourteen

The Truth Shall Set You Free

The Word of God must be our foundation. Apart from it, we cannot be successful (Josh. 1:8). Without it, we cannot be saved (1 Pet. 1:23). Apart from God's Word, we will never find truth (John 17:17). And without God's Word, we cannot know Him (John 1:1).

Much of our society believes that truth is subjective and nothing is absolute, yet they deal in absolutes every day. Math is absolute. No matter what continent you're on, two plus two always equals four. Gravity is another absolute. No matter where you stand on earth, no matter what you throw into the air, gravity will bring it down. Even a statement like "there are no absolutes; truth is relative" is, in itself, an absolute. Unfortunately, many in the body of Christ, especially those in the younger generation, are falling for this foolish idea. We who know the truth are to blame for this.

I recently spoke to a pastor in San Francisco who refused to preach about homosexuality in his church. When I asked him about it, he said, "I want to see these men and women change, and I believe God has given me the wisdom to deal with them. Homosexuals need to know the love of Christ. And I want them to feel free to come to our church and get involved. I want them to be a part, so we just love on them. We don't confront them. We just show them the love of Christ, and I know that love is going to change them."

"I understand what you're saying," I said. "You want to reach homosexuals with the love of Christ, like you were reached. You want them to come to your church and hear the Word. But God's Word says it's the truth that sets people free [John 8:32]."

I continued, "How did you get saved? I bet someone told you about God's love and then confronted you about sin. They explained to you that sin was keeping you from experiencing God, and the only way to get rid of your sin was to believe on Jesus. Am I right?"

The pastor nodded.

"So, if you don't speak the truth and confront the sin of homosexuality, how will these sinners know? And beyond that, what about the young people in your church? If you're not standing up for biblical morality, how will they know what it is? How will they know what true marriage looks like? I can guarantee you, your kids aren't hearing about it at school. They're not hearing it from the secular world. The secular world is very vocal about immorality, about 'tolerance.' But they refuse to tolerate people who don't agree with them. If you don't stand up and speak the truth, then by default, your young people are going to get immorality crammed down their throats."

"I never thought of it that way," the pastor said.

Apparently, a lot of people aren't thinking about it that way. Today, many Christians are being cowed into silence by this thing called political correctness. Political correctness is of the devil. It is a spirit of antichrist. It's not anti-Buddha. It's not anti-Muhammad. It's not anti-homosexual. It's anti-*Christ*. In the United States, it is illegal to discriminate against or persecute every people group except committed Christians. First John 4:3 says:

And every spirit that confesseth not that Jesus Christ is come in the flesh is not of God: and this is that spirit of antichrist, whereof ye have heard that it should come; and even now already is it in the world.

Did you know that Muslim students can wear their garb and say their prayers and hold Islamic meetings in school, but some administrators won't allow Christian kids to do the same thing? A teacher in Ohio actually lost his job because he kept a Bible on his desk. He didn't read it. He didn't force it on his class. He just had it there. Some people said they were offended by it, so he was fired. That's a spirit of antichrist, and it's running rampant in our society.

To avoid this type of persecution, some Christians aren't saying anything about evil. In the name of "love," they refuse to speak truth. But that's wrong. The Bible says, "Be not wise in thine own eyes: fear the LORD, and depart from evil" (Prov. 3:7). It goes on to say, "The fear of the LORD is to hate evil" (Prov. 8:13).

Let love be without dissimulation. Abhor that which is evil; cleave to that which is good.

Romans 12:9

I heard a well-known minister on an international television program responding to some of the social and moral issues of our day. He was asked how Christians should respond to the homosexual agenda, and he responded by saying that Christians weren't the Master Gardener. They should never break off dead limbs; they should just let those limbs fall off naturally. He said his ministry was going to spend its time nurturing and loving the tree, not speaking against sin, and he would let God prune its branches.

But that is not correct. If you truly love a person, you're going to tell them the truth.

Thou shalt not hate thy brother in thine heart: thou shalt in any wise rebuke thy neighbour, and not suffer sin upon him. Thou shalt not avenge, nor bear any grudge against the children of thy people, but thou shalt love thy neighbour as thyself: I am the LORD.

Leviticus 19:17-18

Many people can quote the last part of Leviticus 19:18, "love thy neighbour as thyself," but they don't realize the context that this verse is in. Leviticus says that if you don't rebuke your neighbor when he is in the wrong, then you hate him. If you don't tell him the truth, you don't love him. Part of loving your neighbor is telling him the truth. It's the truth that sets people free (John 8:32).

Late one foggy night I was on a winding, mountain road heading home. There were no streetlights, the moon wasn't out, and it was dark. I could only see a short distance in front of me. Soon a car passed me on the left, slammed on its brakes, and jerked to the right. I could tell it had hit something. As soon as I saw the brake lights pop on, I pulled over and stopped. I ended up on the shoulder right next to this car with its windshield bashed in. The car was in the right lane, I was on the shoulder, and a few feet ahead of us, in the left lane, lay an injured horse. All three lanes were blocked and the man in the other car was obviously injured. Before I knew what was happening, another car came zooming around the bend at sixty miles per hour. Within seconds, this lady in a Suburban hit the horse, and her car went flying through the air. She was a good five or ten feet off the ground and had to have cleared twenty or thirty feet before she came down. Thankfully, she was able to regain control of her vehicle and stop. I assumed she was hurt. There was a bump in the roof of her Suburban where her head may have hit.

I could hear other cars coming up the road, but we were all stopped around a corner, hidden from view. With the fog, there was no way for other cars to see the wreck before it was too late. So I ran down the road and around the corner, and for twenty minutes, I tried to warn cars of the upcoming danger.

I jumped out at every car coming up the pass, waving my arms and shouting. I got honked at, yelled at, and cussed out. People were hitting their brakes and swerving to the side of the road. I'm sure they thought bad things about me. I'm sure they imputed things to me that weren't right. I'm sure they were hating me. Honestly, it would have been much easier to just stay in my car and wait for the police. But if I hadn't gotten out of my car and tried to warn those people, if I hadn't told them the truth, bad things could have happened to them. I would have been more concerned with my reputation than with their lives. I would have loved myself more than I loved my neighbor.

It's not love that sets people free; it's truth (John 8:32). Now, the truth should be spoken in love (Eph. 4:15); it shouldn't be used as a club to beat people. But it's truth that sets people free. As much flack as I got that night as I was flagging down cars, I'm sure a lot of those same people who cussed and reviled me started blessing me when they finally got around the corner and realized I'd saved their lives.

Chapter Fifteen

The Shield of Faith

A person of excellence stands for truth regardless of the consequences. Unfortunately, many Christians today believe that doing the right thing and using their faith should exempt them from the trials and tribulations of life. That's just not true. Jesus said in the world we would have tribulation. Trouble is a fact of life. But then He added, "Be of good cheer; I have overcome the world" (John 16:33).

Believers were never promised an exemption from life's challenges. But we have been given everything we need to overcome!

For whatsoever is born of God overcometh the world: and this is the victory that overcometh the world, even our faith. Who is he that overcometh the world, but he that believeth that Jesus is the Son of God?

1 John 5:4-5

Now thanks be unto God, which always causeth us to triumph in Christ, and maketh manifest the savour of his knowledge by us in every place.

2 Corinthians 2:14

Some people get angry when others promote a life of victory. They don't think total victory is obtainable this side of heaven, and they think teaching others to raise their hopes for victory only leads to disappointment. Of course, it's important for us all to understand that a victorious Christian life is not one without opposition. Satan will shoot his fiery darts at us (Eph. 6:16), but we can overcome. We have been given the shield of faith!

Faith overcomes. It doesn't avoid. Just because Shadrach, Meshach, and Abednego took a stand of faith doesn't mean they were exempt from the fire. The Apostle Paul described faith as a shield (Eph. 6:16), but what use is a shield outside of battle? You don't carry a shield while you're flying a kite. You don't use it as a pillow. That's not its purpose. A shield's purpose is protection. Faith won't necessarily keep you from the fire, but it will protect you in it.

Then was Nebuchadnezzar full of fury, and the form of his visage was changed against Shadrach, Meshach, and Abednego: therefore he spake, and commanded that they should heat the furnace one seven times more than it was wont to be heated. And he commanded the most mighty men that were in his army to bind Shadrach, Meshach, and Abednego, and to cast them into the burning fiery furnace.

Daniel 3:19-20

When Nebuchadnezzar heard that Shadrach, Meshach, and Abednego refused to bow to his image, he was mad. But when they faced Nebuchadnezzar and rebuked him with words of great faith, something demonic rose out of the king. Daniel said, "the form of his visage was changed," and Nebuchadnezzar commanded that the fire be heated seven times hotter than it normally was. How illogical was that? If somebody is thrown into a fire, they're going to burn and eventually die. It doesn't matter how hot the fire is. Nebuchadnezzar's command was of no physical benefit, but it certainly reflected the fact that his anger was out of control. Then Nebuchadnezzar commanded the strongest men in his army to tie up Shadrach, Meshach, and Abednego and throw them into the fire. The fire was so hot, it killed the king's men before they could finish their job!

Then these men were bound in their coats, their hosen, and their hats, and their other garments, and were cast into the midst of the burning fiery furnace. Therefore because the king's commandment was urgent, and the furnace exceeding hot, the flame of the fire slew those men that took up Shadrach, Meshach, and Abednego. And these three men, Shadrach, Meshach, and Abednego, fell down bound into the midst of the burning fiery furnace.

Daniel 3:21-23

In his rage, Nebuchadnezzar sacrificed his strongest men to fix the problem of the three Hebrew children. That was stupid. It's never a good idea to let anger control you. You make stupid decisions in the heat of anger.

Shadrach, Meshach, and Abednego fell bound into the fiery furnace. But praise God, that's not the end of the story!

Then Nebuchadnezzar the king was [astonished] *and rose up in haste, and spake, and said unto his counsellors, Did not we cast three men bound into the midst of the fire? They answered and said unto the king, True, O king. He answered and said, Lo, I see four men loose, walking in the midst of the fire, and they have no hurt; and the form of the fourth is like the Son of God.... And the princes, governors, and captains, and the king's counsellors, being gathered together, saw these men, upon whose bodies the fire had no power, nor was an hair of their head singed, neither were their coats changed, nor the smell of fire had passed on them.*

Daniel 3:24-25 and 27, brackets added

Man, that is awesome! You know, some people don't believe this story really happened, but I believe these things happened exactly the way the Bible describes. I believe these men were thrown into a blazing hot fire that killed their enemies before they could even reach it. I believe Shadrach, Meshach, and Abednego were protected in that fire by faith. All the fire could do was burn off their bonds. They weren't hurt, their clothes weren't burned, and they didn't even smell of smoke! And I believe that a pre-incarnate manifestation of Jesus joined them in that fire, fulfilling God's promise that He would "go before thee; he will be with thee, he will not fail thee, neither forsake thee: fear not, neither be dismayed" (Deut. 31:8).

I know a lot of people would love to see Jesus come down and manifest Himself in the midst of their fiery trials, but how many will use the shield of faith? How many will stand strong like Shadrach, Meshach, and Abednego and not compromise? Often the reason we don't see God miraculously intervene in our situations is because we've compromised. At its heart, compromise is about self-preservation; it does anything to avoid criticism. Compromise exalts man's opinions above God's, and it is ultimately a form of idolatry. God can't reward compromise. That doesn't mean He doesn't love us. That doesn't mean He's mad at us or punishing us. But God can't intervene in our lives without our permission. Faith-filled obedience gives God permission to intervene (Deut. 28:2).

Behold, to obey is better than sacrifice, and to hearken than the fat of rams. For rebellion is as the sin of witchcraft, and stubbornness is as iniquity and idolatry.

1 Samuel 15:22-23

If you want God to intervene on your behalf, if you want to walk through the fire without being burned, you need to obey God. You need to start living by faith, without compromise. You can't follow the crowd. If you want to walk on the water, you have to get out of the boat (Matt. 14:26-29). "But I might sink," you say. Just keep your eyes on Jesus, the Author and the Finisher of your faith (Heb. 12:2), and don't look to the right or to the left. Don't compromise.

God rewards people who stand on conviction, even if they make a mistake. Years ago, the movie *Chariots of Fire* told the story of Olympic athlete Eric Liddell. Liddell was a Scottish citizen born and raised on the mission fields of China. He was also an internationally recognized athlete. The movie depicts Liddell's bid for the gold medal in the 1924 Paris Olympics. Though he was favored to win the 100-meter race, Liddell refused to compete because the preliminaries for the race were held on Sunday. Liddell believed Sunday was the Sabbath, and he did not want to violate God's Word by dishonoring the Sabbath. Technically, Liddell was wrong; biblical Sabbath is from sundown Friday until sundown Saturday. But in Romans, Paul said, "Whatsoever is not of faith is sin" (Rom. 14:23). Because Eric Liddell made his decision by faith—even though he was technically wrong—God blessed him.

Humans exercise a certain amount of faith every day. While driving to work, we all have faith that a two-inch-thick piece of metal and some rubber can stop several thousand pounds' worth of car barreling down the highway at sixty-plus miles an hour. We have faith that other motorists are using those same pieces of rubber to stop their cars at every red light we encounter. When placing an order online, people hand over their money by faith, believing that someone they've never met, whom they could never find in person, will ship their order hundreds of miles across the country in the name of good business. Even something as simple as sitting in a chair takes an element of faith.

But faith is no better than the object in which it is placed. If I want to have great faith, I must first know that the person or thing I'm putting my faith in is trustworthy. For example, if I were to sit on a chair made of cardboard, I would fall flat on my backside, regardless of how much faith I used. In that instance, the object of my faith was faulty. But as believers, the object of our faith—Jesus—is not faulty. Scripture tells us to look "unto Jesus the author and finisher of our faith" (Heb. 12:2). In order to live a life of victory, we must learn to transfer our faith from self to Christ. He is our shield and great reward (Gen. 15:1)!

Chapter Sixteen

Problems Are Not Your Problem

Many people never learn to transfer their faith to Christ. They live life as victims: helpless, whiny, hopelessly out of control. They spend their lives mentally and spiritually curled up in a corner. No one loves them. Everyone is against them. Nothing works in their favor. The past controls them. They think, *If only someone would...if only someone hadn't...if only I could...if only...if only...if only.*

Please let me be clear. If you've found yourself making those kinds of statements, I am not condemning you. I am not trying to make light of anything you've experienced in life. I'm not making light of the wrongs you've suffered. But *everyone* has walked through some version of hell. *Everyone* has been touched by the effects of sin. *Everyone* has a story. Problems are not your problem. Your stinking thinking is your problem.

God created you to live life as an overcomer (Rom. 8:37). The only way to do that is to put your faith in Him. Focus on Him and be conscious of who He is and who He says you can be (2 Pet. 1:3). You can't live a life of victory drowning in "if only." You can't win a battle focused on yourself.

Paul taught that Christians should live their lives dead to self and alive, focused on Christ. Galatians 2:20 says:

I am crucified with Christ: nevertheless I live; yet not I, but Christ liveth in me: and the life which I now live in the flesh I live by the faith of the Son of God, who loved me, and gave himself for me.

A dead person can't feel guilt. They can't feel shame. Dead people can't feel anything. They can't get offended. Neither can they be tempted. If you're constantly dealing with those kinds of emotions, it's because you've not yet crucified yourself with Christ. You are letting your problems take center stage.

Problems do not have to be roadblocks to your success if approached with the right attitude of an excellent spirit. Problems can actually be your ticket to promotion, just as they were for Shadrach, Meshach, and Abednego. After the three Hebrew friends refused to bow to the king's image in Daniel 3, they were thrown into the fire—a problem. But because of their excellent spirits, God showed up and Nebuchadnezzar witnessed a miracle.

Nebuchadnezzar the king was astonished, and rose up in haste, and spake, and said unto his counsellors, Did not we cast three men bound into the midst of the fire? They answered and said unto the king, True, O king. He answered and said, Lo, I see four men loose, walking in the midst of the fire, and they have no hurt; and the form of the fourth is like the Son of God.

Daniel 3:24-25

But notice what happened next:

Then Nebuchadnezzar came near to the mouth of the burning fiery furnace, and spake, and said, Shadrach, Meshach, and Abednego, ye servants of the most high God, come forth, and come hither. Then Shadrach, Meshach, and Abednego, came forth of the midst of the fire.

Daniel 3:26

This is so interesting to me. When the three Hebrew children were loosed, when their ropes burned off and they found they could move about in the fire freely, they stayed. Why didn't they run out? Why didn't they confront the king with his error? Because they had excellent spirits. They really weren't concerned with their problem. They weren't concerned about the king. They were serving God. They didn't let their problem move them.

Then Nebuchadnezzar spake, and said, Blessed be the God of Shadrach, Meshach, and Abednego, who hath sent his angel, and delivered his servants that trusted in him, and have changed the king's word, and yielded their bodies, that they might not serve nor worship any god, except their own God. Therefore I make a decree, That every people, nation, and language, which speak any thing amiss against the God of Shadrach, Meshach, and Abednego, shall be cut in pieces, and their houses shall be made a dunghill: because there is no other God that can deliver after this sort. Then the king promoted Shadrach, Meshach, and Abednego, in the province of Babylon.

Daniel 3:28-30

That's the outcome of excellence! In awe of the way God honored His servants, Nebuchadnezzar promoted Shadrach, Meshach, and Abednego, and publicly proclaimed the supremacy of their God. Their excellent spirits turned a bona fide problem into a steppingstone of promotion (Rom. 8:28).

Throughout history, many, many people have been promoted because of the way they dealt with problems. Look at Joseph, Daniel, and Esther. Consider what you know about George Washington, Einstein, and Martin Luther King, Jr. They were all promoted and revered because they refused to become victims of their circumstances. They knew how to handle problems.

When you think about it, even Stephen, the first martyr of the Christian faith, was promoted because of the way he handled trouble.

And Stephen, full of faith and power, did great wonders and miracles among the people. Then there arose certain of the synagogue, which is called the synagogue of the Libertines, and Cyrenians, and Alexandrians, and of them of Cilicia and of Asia, disputing with Stephen. And they were not able to resist the wisdom and the spirit by which he spake.

Acts 6:8-10

Unable to counter Stephen's excellent spirit, men falsely accused him of blaspheming God. When he was brought to trial before the Sanhedrin, Stephen boldly proclaimed the Word to them. He said, "Ye stiffnecked and uncircumcised in heart and ears, ye do always resist the Holy Ghost: as your fathers did, so do ye…. Who have received the law by the disposition of angels, and have not kept it" (Acts 7:51 and 53). Stephen's inspired words convicted the men of the Sanhedrin, but instead of yielding to the Holy Spirit, they got angry and sent Stephen out to be stoned.

When they heard these things, they were cut to the heart, and they gnashed on him with their teeth. But he, being full of the Holy Ghost, looked up stedfastly into heaven, and saw the glory of God, and Jesus standing on the right hand of God, And said, Behold, I see the heavens opened, and the Son of man standing on the right hand of God. Then they cried out with a loud voice, and stopped their ears, and ran upon him with one accord, And cast him out of the city, and stoned him.

Acts 7:54-58

Notice that Stephen saw Jesus standing at the right hand of God. Normally in Scripture, Jesus is portrayed as being *seated* at the Father's right hand (Luke 22:69, Eph. 1:20, and Col. 3:1). The fact that Stephen saw Jesus standing is significant. I believe Jesus was honoring Stephen. Stephen had not only professed Christ before man, but he also forgave those who were hurting him (Acts 7:60). I believe Jesus was very pleased with Stephen's excellent spirit, and He promoted Stephen, welcoming him to heaven with a standing ovation!

Some things are more important than the status quo, more important than preserving your life. Things like knowing God and pleasing Him should sit at the top of your list of priorities. Someday all of the stuff of this life—all its problems—will not be worth comparing "with the glory which shall be revealed in us" (Rom. 8:18). Heaven is going to be worth it! Don't let momentary troubles persuade you to compromise. Don't let problems turn you into a victim. Remember, you are a child of God (Rom. 8:15), an heir of the promise (Gal. 3:29), and more than a conqueror (Rom. 8:37). You have the power to choose your life (Deut. 30:19). Use your problems as steppingstones. Choose excellence.

Chapter Seventeen

Going Public

Our culture's moral compass is spiraling out of control. While political correctness (the spirit of antichrist) is bullying Christians into silence, politicians are pushing for immoral laws and striving for their own personal agendas. Today when people try to live according to their moral consciences—a freedom granted to them in the United States Bill of Rights—they are taken to court, sued, and stripped of their livelihoods. Some are even jailed.

At the time of this writing, my friend, Dr. James Dobson, is fighting an $800,000 lawsuit for speaking up for truth. In an ungodly society, the truth can be costly, but that doesn't change the fact that it's still the truth. That's one reason I wrote the Declaration of Dependence upon God and His Holy Bible.

The Declaration of Dependence exercises the rights of American citizens to petition their government for moral legislation. It is a document that declares every Christian's right to live according to God's Word. Its signees "respectfully reserve the right" to refuse to participate in or obey unrighteous laws that support abortion and sexual perversion. It proclaims that its signees are committed to "obey God rather than man." The Declaration of Dependence is essentially an act of civil disobedience.

I know a lot of people think we're supposed to obey every rule of man. They think we're supposed to quietly submit to governing authorities and not make a fuss when laws are passed that violate God's Word. But that's not what the Bible teaches.

The Apostle Peter wrote:

Submit yourselves to every ordinance of man for the Lord's sake: whether it be to the king, as supreme; Or unto governors, as unto them that are sent by him for the punishment of evildoers, and for the praise of them that do well. For so is the will of God, that with well doing ye may put to silence the ignorance of foolish men.

1 Peter 2:13-15

Some people have used these verses to say that we're supposed to blindly obey the laws of the land, even if those laws say it's okay to murder babies or for men to marry men and women to marry women. These people say we should obey the rule of law that says it's not okay to pray or read a Bible in public or mention the name of Jesus. But these people forget that this same man—Peter—also defied the Jewish ruling council when they forbade him to preach in the name of Jesus.

In Acts 4, Peter and John were arrested for speaking publicly about Jesus. At this time, the Jewish ruling council was doing everything it could to maintain the status quo. They saw the balance of power shifting away from the temple and the Law, and they were panicking. Many people were converting and becoming disciples of Christ. The apostles were well respected. Miracles happened frequently, proving their words about Jesus. The council feared that the people would stop looking to them for leadership. Not knowing what else to do, they ordered Peter and John to quit preaching Jesus. But Peter and John said:

Whether it be right in the sight of God to hearken unto you more than unto God, judge ye. For we cannot but speak the things which we have seen and heard.

Acts 4:19-20

Later in Acts 5, Peter and some other apostles were arrested again. This time, God miraculously sprung them from jail during the night and instructed them to continue preaching words of life (Acts 5:20). The next morning, when it was discovered that the apostles were no longer prisoners, the council brought them before the high priest. He said:

Did not we straitly command you that ye should not teach in this name? and, behold, ye have filled Jerusalem with your doctrine, and intend to bring this man's blood upon us.

Acts 5:28

Again Peter responded, "We ought to obey God rather than men" (Acts 5:29). Acts goes on to say, "They ceased not to teach and preach Jesus Christ" (Acts 5:42).

Peter and the apostles practiced civil disobedience. They didn't start a war. They didn't begin slandering the council members. But neither did they obey their unrighteous laws. How does that fit with the mandate in 1 Peter 2:13 to submit to governing authorities? Well, the first thing you have to recognize is the difference between submission and obedience. Submission is an attitude of the heart. It is voluntary. Obedience is an action, and it can be forced.

I once heard a cute story about a little kid sitting on the front row of his church. Keeping himself busy playing with cars, this little kid's not-so-quiet game kept interrupting the preacher's sermon. "Vroom, vroom," the boy said, driving his cars back and forth on the pew. "Vrooooooooom!"

Several car races later, the pastor had had enough. "Stop," he shouted at the boy.

"Eeeeerrrrrrrch," the little boy's pretend brakes screeched.

"Sit down," the pastor said. "No more noise!"

The little boy sat down. But as he sat, someone close by heard him mutter, "I may be sitting down on the outside, but I'm standing up on the inside." That little boy obeyed, but he didn't submit.

Obedience can be demanded. It can be coerced. But submission in an attitude of the heart. Peter told us to submit to authority, not necessarily obey it. Peter and the apostles disobeyed their ruling authority, but they did it with an attitude of submission. When they were thrown into jail, Peter and John didn't try to escape. They didn't fight. When they were brought before the council, they didn't throw a fit. They simply recognized that God's authority superseded man's, and they chose publicly to submit to Him. That's what Shadrach, Meshach, and Abednego did. That's what I'm doing with the Declaration. And that's what an excellent spirit will do. A person with an excellent spirit recognizes God's authority, they recognize His Word, and they refuse to exalt man's laws and ideas above God's.

Even Daniel practiced civil disobedience. In Daniel 6, King Darius was tricked into signing a decree that forbade prayer. Members of the cabinet were looking for a way to discredit Daniel and push themselves into the spotlight of the king's favor, so they played to the king's ego and got him to sign their degree into law. The law said that no one could pray to any god or man but the king for thirty days.

> *Then these presidents and princes assembled together to the king, and said thus unto him, King Darius, live for ever. All the presidents of the kingdom, the governors, and the princes, the counsellors, and the captains, have consulted together to establish a royal statute, and to make a firm decree, that whosoever shall ask a petition of any God or man for thirty days, save of thee, O king, he shall be cast into the den of lions. Now, O king, establish the decree, and sign the writing, that it be not changed, according to the law of the Medes and Persians, which altereth not. Wherefore king Darius signed the writing and the decree.*

Daniel 6:6-9

When Daniel heard about this new decree, Scripture says he went to his room, opened his windows, and prayed to God, as was his custom.

Now when Daniel knew that the writing was signed, he went into his house; and his windows being open in his chamber toward Jerusalem, he kneeled upon his knees three times a day, and prayed, and gave thanks before his God, as he did aforetime.

Daniel 6:10

What a bold statement of defiance! Daniel knew about the king's unrighteous law. He knew about the lion's den. He could have prayed to God and stayed committed privately. He didn't have to pray with his windows open. He didn't have to kneel down or face Jerusalem to communicate with God. (There are no formulas for prayer. Prayer can be as simple as meditation—fixing your mind on the Lord [Ps. 5:1 and Is. 26:3]). But Daniel prayed "as he did aforetime." He intentionally made a public display of his faith.

Today, many Christians are told to keep their faith private. They are told it's illegal to practice faith in the marketplace, in the government, or in schools. I've actually heard stories that some schools forbade the use of "Merry Christmas" as a holiday greeting because it was too "religious," while other schools were teaching children Muslim prayers. That's wrong. Yet there are Christians who go along with it, saying, "I'll keep serving the Lord, but I'll just do it privately. I'll worship God at home. I'll serve Him at church, but in public I'll keep my mouth shut." That's wrong, wrong, wrong! Daniel had a government position. He knew about the law, but he didn't hide his devotion to the Lord. He had an excellent spirit, and he took his faith public.

Chapter Eighteen

The Power of God Works

Believing God's Word and not compromising in today's society means that you're going to be different. You're not going to fit in with the crowd. When you have an excellent spirit, you stick out.

For example, a lot of people at work slack off when the boss isn't around. They come in late. They clock out early. If they get a ten-minute break, they take fifteen. They take forever to complete assignments when they're getting paid by the hour. They steal things like stamps, pens, and rubber bands from the office because "no one will ever miss them." Any dead fish can float downstream. Anyone can go with the flow, but it takes a little bit of effort to swim upstream. It takes effort to be excellent. If you want to have an excellent spirit, you're going to have to learn to swim against the stream of culture.

When you start having an excellent spirit and start doing things "heartily, as to the Lord" (Col. 3:23), people will criticize you. Your excellence will make their mediocrity look bad, and rather than climb up to your superior standard, it will be easier to drag you down. Proverbs 13:10 says, "Only by pride cometh contention." When people are contentious toward you, it's because they're prideful and envious.

Daniel's excellent spirit brought him both promotion and enemies.

> *Then this Daniel was preferred above the presidents and princes, because an excellent spirit was in him; and the king thought to set him over the whole realm. Then the presidents and princes sought to find occasion against Daniel concerning the kingdom; but they could find none occasion nor fault; forasmuch as he was faithful, neither was there any error or fault found in him.*

Daniel 6:3-4

Having no error or fault may seem like an unattainable goal, but Daniel reached it. If that can be said of Daniel—an Old Testament saint who wasn't made new with the spirit of Christ living inside of him—what are we capable of (2 Cor. 5:17 and Rom. 8:11)? Remember, this study of an excellent spirit could also be called a study in faithfulness. An excellent spirit is faithful and consistent. It has a moral foundation that doesn't fluctuate or compromise. It does what is right.

Daniel 6:4 says that Daniel's coworkers "sought to find occasion against" him. They became contentious toward Daniel and hated him because his excellent spirit highlighted their mediocrity. The presidents and princes began snooping around to find something they could use against Daniel, but they couldn't find anything, because he was faithful.

Then said these men, We shall not find any occasion against this Daniel, except we find it against him concerning the law of his God.

Daniel 6:5

What a testimony it would be if every Christian lived such an exemplary life that people couldn't find skeletons in their closets to accuse them of wrongdoing! Peter told us to live such good lives among people that "whereas they speak against you as evildoers, they may by your good works, which they shall behold, glorify God" (1 Pet. 2:12). I know many Christians feel condemned over their closets full of skeletons that come from their days before knowing Christ. But praise God, those days are over and those skeletons are forgiven (Rom. 5:6-10)! Life is different now—at least it should be (Titus 3:3-8).

For ye were sometimes darkness, but now are ye light in the Lord: walk as children of light: (For the fruit of the Spirit is in all goodness and righteousness and truth.)

Ephesians 5:8-9

We should be walking as children of the light, in all "goodness and righteousness and truth." When Paul sent money from the believers in Corinth to those in Jerusalem, he asked the church to select people to travel with him so that no one could accuse him of mishandling funds.

> *And not that only, but who was also chosen of the churches to travel with us with this grace, which is administered by us to the glory of the same Lord, and declaration of your ready mind: Avoiding this, that no man should blame us in this abundance which is administered by us: Providing for honest things, not only in the sight of the Lord, but also in the sight of men.*

2 Corinthians 8:19-21

Paul could have taken the money to Jerusalem without the help of the Corinthian people. He didn't need to travel with companions to ensure he did what was right. Paul was an honest man. But he wanted to "provide things honest in the sight of all men" (Rom. 12:17). Another translation says that he attempted to "do things in such a way that everyone [could] see [he was] honorable" (*New Living Translation*, brackets added). Paul knew that even if someone accused him of wrongdoing, God would know his innocence. But, he thought, why put fodder in the rumor mill? Why not live in such a way that no one could accuse him?

That's why I travel with people. I spent years traveling by myself in the early days of my ministry, but people know me now. The ministry is constantly under scrutiny, so I have people travel with me. If someone tries to accuse me of wrongdoing, there are witnesses around who can speak the truth. I'm trying to live in such an exemplary way—not only in the sight of God, but also in the sight of people—that no one can use my life as a reason to malign the Word of God (Titus 2).

Daniel was that kind of guy. He was so faithful that his accusers knew they would never find anything against him unless it concerned his relationship with God. So his accusers came up with a plan to forbid prayer, but Daniel was not afraid. He stood his ground.

Now when Daniel knew that the writing was signed, he went into his house; and his windows being open in his chamber toward Jerusalem, he kneeled upon his knees three times a day, and prayed, and gave thanks before his God, as he did aforetime. Then these men assembled, and found Daniel praying and making supplication before his God. Then they came near, and spake before the king concerning the king's decree; Hast thou not signed a decree, that every man that shall ask a petition of any God or man within thirty days, save of thee, O king, shall be cast into the den of lions? The king answered and said, The thing is true, according to the law of the Medes and Persians, which altereth not. Then answered they and said before the king, That Daniel, which is of the children of the captivity of Judah, regardeth not thee, O king, nor the decree that thou hast signed, but maketh his petition three times a day.

Daniel 6:10-13

Daniel was seized and thrown into a den of lions.

Then the king commanded, and they brought Daniel, and cast him into the den of lions. Now the king spake and said unto Daniel, Thy God whom thou servest continually, he will deliver thee. And a stone was brought, and laid upon the mouth of the den; and the king sealed it with his own signet, and with the signet of his lords; that the purpose might not be changed concerning Daniel.

Daniel 6:16-17

I'm sure Daniel's accusers were giddy at this point. I'm sure they thought they'd won. But instead of the lions attacking eighty-year-old Daniel, God supernaturally protected him.

Then the king arose very early in the morning, and went in haste unto the den of lions. And when he came to the den, he cried with a lamentable voice unto Daniel: and the king spake and said to Daniel, O Daniel, servant of the living God, is thy God, whom thou servest continually, able to deliver thee from the lions? Then said Daniel unto the king, O king, live for ever. My God hath sent his angel, and hath shut the lions' mouths, that they have not hurt me: forasmuch as before him innocency was found in me; and also before thee, O king, have I done no hurt.

Daniel 6:19-22

That is awesome! Daniel was a man of excellence. He didn't hide his faith. His life became such a public declaration of the goodness of God that even the king said:

[Daniel's God] *is the living God, and stedfast for ever, and his kingdom that which shall not be destroyed, and his dominion shall be even unto the end. He delivereth and rescueth,*

and he worketh signs and wonders in heaven and in earth,
who hath delivered Daniel from the power of the lions.

Daniel 6:26-27, brackets added

If we're going to have excellent spirits, we have to start publicly displaying our faith. That doesn't mean we go out looking for ways to draw attention to ourselves, but we should willingly take a stand for truth and boldly proclaim the goodness of God at every opportunity. Paul said, "I am not ashamed of the gospel of Christ: for it is the power of God unto salvation to every one that believeth" (Rom. 1:16). We should not be ashamed of the truth. If we are the redeemed, we should be saying so (Ps. 107:2)!

Conclusion

Though Babylon viewed Daniel, Hananiah, Mishael, and Azariah's heritage as Jews as their greatest weakness, God turned that "weakness" into their greatest strength. Daniel and his friends knew who they were. They knew their God-identity. They understood the power of humility. They knew God was their source. And they stood for truth without compromise in both their private lives and in the public square. They had excellent spirits.

You see, excellence is the key to promotion. But an excellent spirit doesn't just happen. You have to choose to develop the characteristics I've been talking about and combine them to see success. Excellence isn't just about identity. It's not just humility. It's not just about standing for truth. Excellence is all these things.

You have to know who you are in Christ. That's where your potential lies. You have to have a personal relationship with God and His Word. You can't limit yourself to only those things you can see in the natural realm. You also have to be humble. You can't just do your own thing. You have to be God-dependent. You can't live life stuck in the rut of pleasing man. You have to recognize that God is the ultimate authority. He is your source.

If you want to have an excellent spirit, you can't compromise. You must hold on to your convictions no matter the cost. Society's truths, their convictions, change to suit society. But God's Word never changes, and a person of excellence builds their life on that surety. They aren't worried about the future because they know God is faithful.

A person with an excellent spirit is not ashamed of his faith. He isn't worried over criticism or persecution. When trouble comes his way, he doesn't hide in his home with the windows closed. A person with an excellent spirit meets challenges head on. In everything, he seeks to honor and obey God rather than man.

But you can't just pick and choose the parts of excellence you like, ignore the rest, and expect God to promote you. You have to take all the characteristics I've talked about and combine them to see the benefits of an excellent spirit. The person who does these things, like Daniel did, can expect to be honored by God and promoted among people.

For them that honour me I will honour, and they that despise me shall be lightly esteemed.

1 Samuel 2:30

For promotion cometh neither from the east, nor from the west, nor from the south. But God is the judge: he putteth down one, and setteth up another.

Psalm 75:6-7

Receive Jesus as Your Savior

Choosing to receive Jesus Christ as your Lord and Savior is the most important decision you'll ever make!

God's Word promises, **"That if thou shalt confess with thy mouth the Lord Jesus, and shalt believe in thine heart that God hath raised him from the dead, thou shalt be saved. For with the heart man believeth unto righteousness; and with the mouth confession is made unto salvation"** (Romans 10:9,10). **"For whosoever shall call upon the name of the Lord shall be saved"** (Romans 10:13).

By His grace, God has already done everything to provide salvation. Your part is simply to believe and receive.

Pray out loud: Jesus, I confess that You are my Lord and Savior. I believe in my heart that God raised You from the dead. By faith in Your Word, I receive salvation now. Thank You for saving me.

The very moment you commit your life to Jesus Christ, the truth of His Word instantly comes to pass in your spirit. Now that you're born again, there's a brand-new you.

Receive the
Holy Spirit

As His child, your loving heavenly Father wants to give you the supernatural power you need to live a new life.

For every one that asketh receiveth; and he that seeketh findeth; and to him that knocketh it shall be opened... how much more shall your heavenly Father give the Holy Spirit to them that ask him?

Luke 11:10-13

All you have to do is ask, believe, and receive!

Pray: *Father, I recognize my need for Your power to live a new life. Please fill me with Your Holy Spirit. By faith, I receive it right now. Thank You for baptizing me. Holy Spirit, You are welcome in my life.*

Congratulations—now you're filled with God's supernatural power.

Some syllables from a language you don't recognize will rise up from your heart to your mouth. (1 Corinthians 14:14.) As you speak them out loud by faith, you're releasing God's power from within and building yourself up in the spirit. (1 Corinthians 14:4.) You can do this whenever and wherever you like.

It doesn't really matter whether you felt anything or not when you prayed to receive the Lord and His Spirit. If you believed in your heart that you received, then God's Word promises you did. **"Therefore I say unto you, What things soever ye desire, when ye pray, believe that ye receive them, and ye shall have them"** (Mark 11:24). God always honors His Word—believe it!

Please contact me and let me know that you've prayed to receive Jesus as your Savior or be filled with the Holy Spirit. I would like to rejoice with you and help you understand more fully what has taken place in your life. I'll send you a free gift that will help you understand and grow in your new relationship with the Lord. Welcome to your new life!

About the Author

Andrew's life was forever changed the moment he encountered the supernatural love of God on March 23, 1968. You could say his theology was transformed overnight. Andrew went from seeing God as someone from whom he had to earn approval, to a Father who accepted him on an unconditional basis and who greatly desired fellowship with him. The author of more than thirty books, Andrew has made it his mission for nearly five decades to change the way the world sees God, by focusing on God's love and grace.

Andrew's vision is to go as far and deep with the Gospel as possible. His message goes *far* through the *Gospel Truth* television and radio program, which is available to nearly half the world's population. Additionally, he has an extensive library of teaching materials in print, audio, and video—most of which can be downloaded for free from his website: **www.awmi.net**. To date, his ministry has distributed millions of free teaching materials globally.

The message goes *deep* through discipleship—training, equipping, and mentoring the next generation of leaders through Charis Bible College, founded in 1994. There are currently more than seventy Charis campuses and over 6,000 students worldwide, set to carry on the same mission of changing the way the world sees God.

What God can do through one person whose vision has been changed to see Him properly is the story of Andrew's legacy.

To contact Andrew Wommack please write, e-mail, or call:

Andrew Wommack Ministries, Inc.
P.O. Box 3333
Colorado Springs, CO 80934-3333
E-mail: info@awmi.net
Helpline Phone (orders and prayer):
719-635-1111
Hours: 4:00 AM to 9:30 PM MST

Andrew Wommack Ministries of Europe
P.O. Box 4392
WS1 9AR Walsall
England
E-mail: enquiries@awme.net
U.K. Helpline Phone (orders and prayer):
011-44-192-247-3300
Hours: 5:30 AM to 4:00 PM GMT

Or visit him on the Web at: www.awmi.net

The Harrison House Vision

Proclaiming the truth and the power

Of the Gospel of Jesus Christ

With excellence;

Challenging Christians to

Live victoriously,

Grow spiritually,

Know God intimately.

Fast. Easy.
Convenient.

For the latest Harrison House product information and author news, look no further than your computer. All the details on our powerful, life-changing products are just a click away. New releases, E-mail subscriptions, testimonies, monthly specials — find it all in one place. Visit harrisonhouse.com today!

harrisonhouse